HIDDEN ABERDEENSHIRE
The Coast

DR FIONA-JANE BROWN

BLACK & WHITE PUBLISHING

First published 2014
by Black & White Publishing Ltd
29 Ocean Drive, Edinburgh EH6 6JL

1 3 5 7 9 10 8 6 4 2   14 15 16 17

ISBN: 978 1 84502 757 5

ALBA | CHRUTHACHAIL

Typeset by Creative Link, North Berwick
Printed and bound in Poland
www.hussarbooks.pl

To the folk of coastal Aberdeenshire, for sharing their reminiscences and tales. May the storytelling tradition continue in every future generation.

Contents

Introduction

As a native of Aberdeenshire, I was aware of some good stories that I had never seen in print, but it turned out that my home county was the source of many fascinating tales. *Hidden Aberdeenshire: The Coast* is thus a journey through the lives of the locals, who have shared wonderful gems from their oral history – events that have been passed down through many generations – and yet are still as vibrant as when they were first told. Stories new to me included the connection with the wartime code breaker Alan Turing and Aberdour's ruined kirk, how a 'duck' helped the war effort at Crimond, and how one churchman's confidence in divine protection saved him from a sticky end at Lochee Brig near Inverallochy Castle. There were simply too many to choose from, thus I hope this little selection will encourage readers to go and find out more for themselves.

My definition of Aberdeenshire is the historical one, bounded by Aberdeen City to the south, and Banffshire to the north-west. This was a deliberate choice to allow scope for more detailed work on the other parts of modern Aberdeenshire in the future.

Don't forget that the walking tours in Aberdeen are still running. Consult the website for further details: http://www.hiddenaberdeen.co.uk.

FORMARTINE

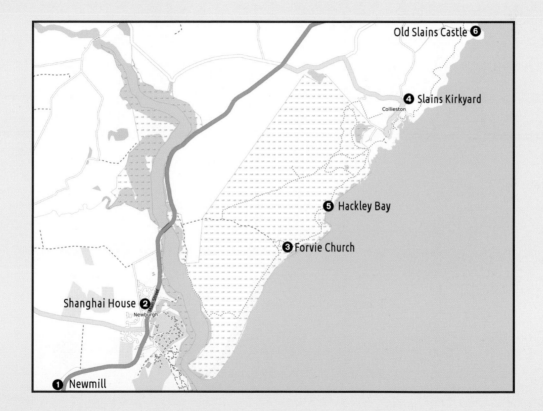

1 Newmill

2 Shanghai House
Newburgh

3 Forvie Church

4 Slains Kirkyard
Collieston

5 Hackley Bay

6 Old Slains Castle

1. The Farmer's Son Who Met Lawrence of Arabia – James McBey, Newmill, Newburgh

The tall, broad-shouldered farmer's son from Newburgh had come so far from the blacksmith's shop where he was born. Now he stood near one of his own oil paintings displayed in London's Royal Academy, watching a visitor – a small man who looked uncomfortable in a suit – study it intently. James McBey, who had been an official artist in the Great War, was now living in a sumptuous house in London once owned by the author John Galsworthy.

Feeling he recognised the scruffy character before him, he approached the man, and to McBey's surprise, it was the very subject of the painting, T.E. Lawrence, the hero of the Egyptian campaigns. Lawrence, who had inspired the Arabs and helped them win back their traditional lands, did not court celebrity, just as McBey hardly spoke of his art. Looking out of place in civilian clothes, Lawrence said sadly, 'Yes, Mr McBey, our last meeting was in rather different circumstances.'

James McBey, born out of wedlock to Annie Gillespie and James McBey of Mains of Foveran, had experienced a terribly inhibited childhood. His mother, suffering the onset of blindness, seemed to resent him and did all she could to prevent him making friends. He loved his grandmother, the blacksmith's wife, the first of the family to see his fledgling drawings, but Annie hated any show of affection, leaving her son constantly disappointed. James' only joy at school had been geography, when he discovered a facility for drawing maps, from which came his ability to sketch landscapes and people. At fourteen he began work in the North of Scotland Bank, a career he did not relish, but living in Aberdeen allowed him access to the Central Library where James devoured every art book he could. He taught himself printmaking and was soon spending all his spare time making etchings. Indeed his first attempt to be taken seriously by the art world was when he sent two works to the Royal Scottish Academy. Only one, a print of Old Torry, was accepted for exhibition in 1905. Twelve years later, James McBey would be in the desert with General Allenby, T.E. Lawrence and the Egypt Expeditionary Force, recording the struggle against the Turks, Germany's allies in World War I.

McBey's war material was a return to those early days of sketching quickly, creating what later critics would call 'a comprehensive and honest record' of the conflict. Prof. Mario Minichiello, former war artist in twenty-first-century Afghanistan, believes the simplicity of the images 'renders the figures the subject of detailed scrutiny, and . . . I believe gives him his uniqueness as an artist.'

When James met T.E. Lawrence again it was on the brink of his success. Both had been enchanted by the desert landscape, and James would eventually settle in Morocco. He returned to Newburgh twice more before his death in 1959. Perhaps his love of the North African sand dunes was inspired by those near his childhood home, but abroad he was finally free of his tragic beginnings.

The site of Newmill Smithy, Newburgh

2. The Shipmaster's Home –
Shanghai House, Main Street, Newburgh

'It's a girl!' the ship's surgeon informed Captain John Thomson of the *Omar Pasha*, the largest of Aberdeen's clippers, which had been launched two years previously. The child was the captain's daughter, Eleanor. She was born to his wife, also Eleanor, who had accompanied him on the voyage from Sydney, Australia. In 1861, young Eleanor Ann Thomson, the child born at sea, was recorded as living in Newburgh with her siblings, aunt and grandmother, when her father died on board his famous ship returning from Down Under. Her mother's name is conspicuously absent from the census, thus Eleanor Thomson Sr must have been on board with her husband.

In happier times, John and his wife had commissioned a grand two-storey house in Newburgh, set back from Main Street in a large garden. Built in 1850 while Captain

Thomson was employed by the Aberdeen White Star Line, it was christened Shanghai House, after one of his favourite ports of call. Four years later, constructed in Walter Hood's Fittie shipyard, the *Omar Pasha* was

launched, destined to be Thomson's new ship to engage the Australian and Chinese trade. Since the repeal of British navigation laws in 1849, America had seized the chance to compete with the UK; thus the battle of the clippers began. Aberdeen's were the best and fastest in the world. Eleanor Ann's birth occurred when the *Omar Pasha* had a cargo of gold dust and sovereigns worth over £10,000, but usually the ship carried more mundane items as well as wealthy passengers keen to visit exotic countries. Thomson's seafaring skills were put to the test in January 1860 when the ship was trapped for a fortnight on the English Channel in bitter storms. However, the fact that he still reached Cape Otway in Victoria, Australia, in 71 days, making the Equator in only 15 days, proved that ship and captain were perfectly suited to the job.

John Thomson's concern for his ship's well-being would prove his undoing the following year. Leaving Sydney in February 1861 for London, the ship had to sail across the Pacific via South America, as neither the Panama nor Suez Canals had been built at that time. Passing through the Southern Ocean, Captain Thomson was very perturbed to discover floating pack ice and, according to one observer, the captain 'never left the deck for eight or ten days and nights'. Ignoring the medical officer's warnings to wear warm clothing, the captain kept company with his crew on every watch. Finally Thomson caught a cold, which he fought fiercely. The infection 'settled on his lungs and carried him off'. He died at the beginning of March, and the twenty-two-year-old first mate, John Allen, was left with the onerous task of bringing the clipper safely home. The *Sydney Morning Herald* noted that Thomson had been 'universally liked for his generous and good-hearted nature'. How desperate it must have been for Mrs Thomson returning to Shanghai House and having to tell her children their father had died at sea, latitude 58° S, longitude 98° W, just west of Cape Horn.

3. Curse or Coincidence? – The Sands of Forvie

'The scene was more in accordance with the desolation of an African wilderness than the blue hills and green valleys of my native Caledonia. No trace of human habitation could be seen,' wrote an anonymous correspondent to *The Aberdeen Magazine* in 1832. The 'vast Sahara' they described was the Sands of Forvie, today a nature reserve buzzing with bird life.

Many legends have spawned as a result of the village of Forvie's burial in the dunes, which occurred many centuries ago. Sixteenth-century hellfire preacher Rev. Masson declared that Forvie's inhabitants had been ignorant Papists punished by a reforming deity. In a lesser-known tale, a strange minister comes to Forvie and, discovering the villagers love nothing more than to gossip about their neighbours, turns them all against each other, while secretly killing local virgins to aid his black arts. He is eventually revealed as the Devil

in disguise, who calls upon the four winds to destroy Forvie and its sinful parishioners. Lastly, the most widely accepted story features three spinster sisters. A male relative, determined to have their inheritance, contrives to cast them out to sea in a leaky boat. The girls, like Macbeth's witches, issue a curse against the village for ignoring their plight: 'Let nocht bee funde in Furvye's glebys / Bot thystl, bente and sande.'

But the community at Forvie did have a long life. The Ythan river had supported Mesolithic hunter-gatherers with a vast supply of fish, evidenced by fragments of flint spearheads and fishbones in ancient midden piles. 'Kerb cairns' discovered among the dunes showed that the earliest farmers buried their dead at Forvie 5,000 ago. Further traces demonstrate that this coastal area was continuously inhabited for generations before the sands forced out the medieval crofters in the fifteenth century. The ruins of the chapel – a tiny building by modern standards – can still be found amongst the marram grass that dominates the land, knitting the sand together to create fertile ground. The chapel was in existence from the thirteenth century, according to the Chartulary of Arbroath, a list of Scotland's religious foundations, possibly on an earlier monastic site dedicated to Adomnán, Abbot of Iona and St Columba's biographer. Archaeologists have found contemporary remains of huts constructed from stone and clay around the chapel, as well as the evidence of daily life, such as a spindle whorl, pottery and metal coins.

How did the sands gobble up a whole village? The truth is as mundane as the storm which buried the original Chapel of St Olaf at Cruden Bay. Meteorological records show that in August 1413 a combination of extreme tides and high winds blew the sands from the beach strand at Forvie inland, creating a 100-foot-high dune that smothered the village. For a millennium the dunes had been stable, but by the end of the 1400s, the sand had moved almost 1,500 feet inland, rendering the area completely inhospitable. Thus the author of Forvie's fate was not the Devil, the Almighty, nor angry heiresses, but Nature at its fiercest.

4. Philip Kennedy, Smuggler and Folk Hero – Slains Kirk Cemetery, Collieston

'God send us men like Kennedy, who for true manhood bled,' runs a line in a poem lamenting the death of Philip Kennedy, farmer and smuggler in the parish of Slains near Collieston.

The whole Aberdeenshire coastline was a magnet for the illicit movement of goods following the Act of Union in 1707, as the duty on intoxicating liquor was hiked up to finance England's debts. It was believed by the authorities that 10,000 gallons of spirits were landed illegally every month here. The hamlet of Oldcastle was so notorious a site for burying smuggled goods that once during a dance at a nearby farm the ground gave way beneath the crowd, casting the unfortunate dancers in amongst hidden barrels of French and Dutch contraband.

Almost a century later, in Kennedy's day, the situation had not changed. The Collieston area abounded in caves, all on the edge of nearby farms, such as Clochtow and East Bridgend, close neighbours of the Kennedys at Ward of Slains. On the night in question, 19 December 1798, Philip and his brother John – both strapping lads – waited in the dark at Cransdale Head just outside Collieston. Well-acquainted with the precariousness of their position, the Kennedy brothers carried stout wooden staffs weighted with lead; twentieth-century robbers would carry a smaller version called a cosh. Philip and John were not going to mess about if disturbed.

The cargo, sixteen ankers (or 160 gallons) of Holland gin, was brought ashore by the crew of a Dutch lugger. The brothers and a few of their farm servants would transport the barrels up to the Ward and conceal them until their buyer came to call. However, someone in the party had 'shopped' the Kennedys, as a few minutes later they were met by three excisemen, armed with cutlasses. The 'gaugers', as they were known, clearly expected the men's arrival. A fight ensued and Philip Kennedy's servants scattered like worried sheep, leaving only him and John, who was in danger of being overpowered by one exciseman named Anderson. Philip tripped up the latter's colleagues and held them down with his considerable strength.

Anderson, having already struck John down with his sword, demanded that Philip release his colleagues. Philip refused. Anderson swung the cutlass, bringing the curved blade down on what the poem described as 'the loftiest head . . . in all broad Buchan's land', leaving a wide open wound. The official panicked and ran. The bleeding farmer hauled himself to his feet and staggered off to fetch aid for his brother. A mile further on, Philip crashed through the door of Kirkton

farmhouse and collapsed on a wooden settle, or *deas*. As his neighbours attempted to bind his head, he gasped with his last breath, 'If a' had been as true as I, I'd nae be dying now!'

Unsurprisingly, Anderson was acquitted of murder. Kennedy's grave in Slains Kirkyard is the only physical reminder of his existence, but he is enshrined in folk memory as a hero defying a bullying authority.

5. Clifftop Rescue* – Hackley Bay

Collieston had another winter's tale which made a hero out of Dick Ingram, a local man in his early twenties who lived at Cluny Cottages. His neighbour, George Ross, aged twelve at the time, tells the story of how Dick earned a medal, which was later presented by no less a dignitary than His Majesty, George VI.

Young George heard the warning rocket go up near his home on a wintry Sunday night, about 11pm, in early 1943. Knowing that his father, a member of the local volunteer coastguard, was ill, George got dressed and joined the crew to aid a ship which had run aground at Oldcastle. Little help was needed, and by morning George was home again. A few hours later, however, the real adventure began.

Another distress flare had been spotted towards Newburgh: Dick Ingram had discovered the sad sight of the wrecked forecastle of the tiny *Lesrix*, a coaster which had broken in half on treacherous rocks at Hackley Bay. As they would later learn, ten of the crew had been washed away. George retrieved all the remaining ropes from the coastguard's apparatus shed and met Dick above the bay. The conditions were impossible for any sea rescue, as George recalled the 'mountainous waves' and 'smore drifts'. But Dick was undaunted. He and George succeeded in throwing a line to the four survivors huddled on the wreck. George secured a stronger rope to a stout rock and Dick tied the other end around his waist before climbing down to the shore.

George described the heart-stopping view of the exhausted sailors trying to clamber from the *Lesrix* to Dick's outstretched arms. The gap between boat and shore was being drenched by waves. The first mate and aged captain were washed away, but to George's

relief, the backwash spewed them back onto a ledge near Dick. Having rescued all the men, Dick helped them crawl up the cliff. 'I still can see it,' George said thoughtfully when interviewed in 2007. The rest of the coastguard team arrived to help the men to safety, and George ran home to tell his father. 'Dad didn't like the sea, but I think he wis pleased,' George recalled.

However, George's headmaster was not interested that his pupil had missed a day's school to take part in a rescue, and reprimanded him in front of everyone.

But George's happiest moment was when his brave friend went to London to receive his medal: 'I can still feel his footsteps going past the house when he wis leaving.' Dick's medal was inscribed 'for Gallantry in Saving Life at Sea', but poor George got nothing. The coastguard crew felt he was too young and should not really have been involved.

The first mate of the *Lesrix* stayed for two weeks with the Ingrams, vainly searching the coast for the bodies of his lost crew. There was 'nothing left' of the *Lesrix*; the men were never found, but George Ross would never forget his cliff-top adventure of January 1943.

* This story was part of an interview for the Formartine Oral History Project, which the author co-ordinated in 2006–08.

6. A Different Gunpowder Plot – Old Slains Castle

Slains Castle, a spectacular ruin perched on a jagged coastline, is locally associated with Bram Stoker's horror tale *Dracula*. But there was another Slains, of which only crumbling fragments remain in a remote hamlet to the south of Cruden Bay.

Oldcastle, now a picturesque former fishing village, is dominated by this remnant of the fortress given in 1308 to Sir Gilbert Hay, Earl of Errol, by Robert the Bruce to recognise the former's loyalty. Almost three centuries later, Slains would be blasted to smithereens by gunpowder purchased by James VI, as a punishment to the ninth earl, Francis Hay, for a treasonable act. What terrible crime had this nobleman committed to merit such royal vengeance?

Hay, like most of his neighbours, was a Catholic, and wished to restore his country and monarchy to its former religion. After the execution of Mary, Queen of Scots, all attention was focused on her young son, James Stuart, by both Catholic and Protestant factions; but the teenage king, who would later be called 'the wisest fool in Christendom', demonstrated his political savvy even then.

Despite trying to remain on good terms with both sides, things became extremely complicated for King James in 1592. George Kerr, a Scots priest, was arrested aboard a ship bound for Spain, having in his possession certain 'blanks' signed by three prominent Catholic nobles, including Francis Hay, kindly addressing Philip II, the Spanish monarch. The empty letters were thought to contain messages written in invisible ink outlining a plot to invade Britain. Kerr confessed that one letter was from James VI himself, discussing how Spain could help the Scots monarch gain the English throne from Protestant Elizabeth I.

This left James in a quandary. The Church leaders demanded that the named earls be tried in court, and even the English queen's ambassadors wanted the men imprisoned for treason. So James demanded that Hay and co-conspirators William Douglas and George Gordon, Earl of Huntly, come before him and explain themselves, which they refused to do and went into hiding. James' forces, led by the Earl of Argyll, suffered ignominious defeat by the smaller Catholic army at the Battle of Glenlivet in 1594. Hay feared the king's wrath and fled to Europe, but returned in secret in 1597. In order to gain a pardon, which was readily given, Hay claimed he had embraced Protestantism.

The destruction of Old Slains says more about the young king's shrewd actions than it does about Hay's loyalty. Was this a demonstration to Elizabeth I of his commitment to a Protestant succession, now she

knew the Tudor line was at an end? Or was it to convince the churchmen that James was not involved in a Jesuit plot involving the Pope and Philip of Spain? Whatever the case, Francis Hay built his new home out of sight of the old one. Four centuries would elapse before a Hay re-occupied Old Slains; in the 1960s, Countess Diana Hay lived in the cottage right next to the castle ruins until her death in 1978.

CRUDEN BAY & BODDAM

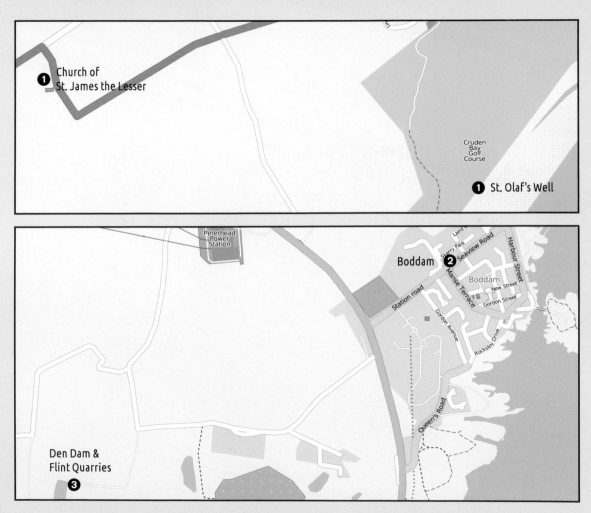

① Church of
St. James the Lesser

Cruden
Bay
Golf
Course

① St. Olaf's Well

Peterhead
Power
Station

Laird's
Sherry Park

Boddam **②** Seaview Road

Harbour Street

Station road

Manse Terrace

Boddam

New Street

Gordon Street

Gordon Avenue

Rocksley Drive

Queen's Road

Den Dam &
Flint Quarries

③

1. Slaughter of the Danes – The Battle of Cruden Bay

'Cuir críoch na Dane!' screamed Malcolm II's warriors as they prepared to attack the Scandinavian forces of Sweyn, King of Denmark, in 1012AD. Many scholars have argued that *'Croij Dane!'* – a phonetic rendering of the Scots Gaelic, which literally translates as 'Die Dane!' – is the origin of the name *Cruden Bay*. The Bay of Ardendraught, the reputed site of this conflict, already had a Norse name, meaning 'Old Dane's Road'. Malcolm II, King of Alba, ruled a much smaller Scotland than we know today, stretching only as far as Moray in the north and Midlothian in the south. He had already attempted to secure control over the Western and Northern Isles by marrying his youngest daughter to Sigurd, Earl of Orkney. Her sisters were married to the Abbot of Dunkeld and Mormaer of Moray, which further increased the king's influence. But the Danes were a nuisance, and Malcolm's men were spoiling for a fight. Sweyn sent his second son, Canute, later the famed king of England, with an army intent on Scottish invasion.

Malcolm wisely engaged in guerrilla tactics, harassing the Danish army, much to his men's annoyance. Eventually these angry Celts bore down their leader's resistance and had a decisive showdown with the seventeen-year-old Dane and his forces. According to Alexander Smith's *A New History of Aberdeenshire*, the 'hottest part of the conflict is supposed to have been on the plain skirting the bay and along the valley, about half a mile in breadth', where stands the golf course laid out by GNSR five years before the great railway hotel was built in 1899.

The battle was a bloody one; the Scots were the victors, but their dead almost equalled those of the Danes. Malcolm and Canute agreed a truce, the terms of which included the total withdrawal of Danish forces from Scotland, and the founding of a chapel near the battlefield to commemorate the dead of both sides. Thus St Olaf's Chapel came into being. Historians argue that as the patron saint of Norway was not even canonised until 1164, the dedication must have come much later. A granite font was installed in the chapel, and it is this relic which would prove the last link to the ancient battle.

Malcolm II likely agreed to the chapel as a form of atonement for the deaths of so many. Devout Catholic he might have been, but that did not stop him from having his nephew assassinated to ensure the succession of his grandson, Duncan, setting up later conflict with his younger grandson, Macbeth.

The font, restored by local priests James Pratt and

Stewart Forbes, now stands in the sanctuary of St James the Lesser, Cruden Bay's Episcopal Church. It is a huge hollowed-out stone, clearly a work of more primitive masonry, but is still used in baptismal services, a symbol of cleansing, as the prayers of the early priests would have been for Cruden's Dark Age battlefield.

2. 'Fa Hung The Monkey?' – The Boddamers and That Infamous Legend

There wis a ship cam' roon the coast
And a' the men in her wis lost
Burrin' the monkey that clam the post
So the Boddamers hinged the monkey-O

Except the Boddamers don't want to take the blame for animal cruelty; yet, the supporters of Hartlepool United FC are quite happy to be known as 'Monkey-Hangers', so the question is, who *did* hang the monkey, if he was hanged at all?

In Aberdeenshire, the monkey legend and the song have been traditionally associated with wrecking activities in coastal villages. George Cordiner, the son of a Boddamer, recalled the details: 'Aa the folk along the Buchan coast, even the Squire o the villages they were in, they were aa wreckers, . . . they hadna

lighthouses, they put up false beacons and the ship would be wrecked, but the Law wis, . . . ye were allowed tae strip a boat, tak onything aff ye wanted, but nae while there was a living soul aboard, but this ship, the only livin thing aboard was the monkey, that climbed the mast tae get away fae the water, and tae get ower this rule, they hung the monkey!' The Scottish Court of Session had indeed passed such a law in 1674, which was later repealed. It lingered in folk memory, however, providing the perfect excuse to 'salvage' from wrecks, as the wily Eriskay islanders did with the cargo of the S.S. *Politician* in 1941.

But the song, traditionally sung to the tune 'The Tinkers' Wedding', spawned several versions, from Cullen, Glasgow, Greenock – one involving a uniform-clad baboon from Tyneside – and then Liverpudlian

musical performer Ned Corvan's 'The Fishermen Hung the Monkey-O'. The latter not only laid the charge against the fishermen of Seaton Carew, an ancient district of Hartlepool, but also poked fun at the fact they thought the beast was a French spy! A twenty-first-century version is sung today by the football supporters whose mascot is a monkey called 'H'Angus'. Folk singer Stewart McFarlane suggests that there may be a darker strand to the monkey legend: 'powder monkeys' were young boys who filled the cannons on warships with gunpowder. Perhaps the fishers of Hartlepool really did hang a Frenchman after all.

But the Boddamers' reputation as wreckers was certainly fuelled by their bitter rivals in the planned village of Burnhaven. A retired fisherman whose grandparents were products of the opposing villages recalls how a ship grounded at Sandford Bay between the two was stripped of its booty by 'Burnies' (i.e.

inhabitants of Burnhaven), yet the blame put on the Boddamers, as the goods were hidden in The Dens, an area near Stirlinghill, outside Boddam. Such stories suggest that the 'monkey' never existed. It was merely an urban legend designed to make the Boddam fishers seem lawless and ignorant. A similar slur was raised against the lost village of Botany by its neighbours. Yet, despite the passing of time, native Boddamers still bristle at the question, 'Fa hinged the monkey?' A smart rejoinder often follows, 'Why, have ye lost yer brither?'

3. Knappers and Boatie-Makers – The Den Dam, Boddam

Older than man are the rocks that lie buried under our feet: the Buchan Gravel Ridge is one such example. Formed in the Pliocene period, almost 5,000 million years ago, it proved a boon to our Neolithic ancestors farming in Aberdeenshire around 3,000 BC. The ridge, stretching from Den of Boddam to Moss of Cruden, provided a rich source of flint to the extent that these Stone Age agriculturalists actively worked the area, creating Britain's first ever flint mines.

Flint is an oddity in itself, formed from chalky rocks. The Buchan Ridge had no chalk, but contained a top layer of gravely, gritty material likely left over from the movement of ancient glaciers, the stuff geologists call moraine. The early farmers had to scrape out pits to get through the moraine to the real treasure, grey or toffee-brown cobbles of siliceous material.

In the hands of an expert 'knapper' these cobbles would be transformed into razor-sharp tools for tilling the land, harvesting the crops and building houses out of wood. Flint ripples when struck to create a 'conchoidal fracture' with edges sharper than steel. The knapper knew exactly where and how hard to strike the flint. Using smaller strikes, he would shape his tool of choice. His hunter-gatherer ancestors would have made arrowheads capable of felling wild deer at great distances. Archaeologists discovered from the fragmentary evidence that some of The Den's knappers used anvils, possibly made of nearby Peterhead granite from Stirlinghill.

Fast forward to the nineteenth-century agricultural improvers who utilised The Den stream to create a reservoir for the local mill, sometime between 1840

and 1868, when the 'Mill Dam' appears first on the OS map. The farmers sunk wells to further benefit from this innovation.

The Den Dam was also the site of the annual model boat races held by the fisherfolk of Boddam. Like the flute bands of Invercairn and St Combs, this was an initiative of the Temperance Movement, encouraging the young men to develop model-making as a serious hobby rather than frequenting the alehouse. These were scale models of contemporary fishing boats, the 'Fifies', which had the added bonus of training many an apprentice carpenter. The late Jim 'Sodger' Reid, whose grandparents lived in Boddam, joined in the model-making and races. He recalled being taught by local sailmaker Keith Hutton to make an aerodynamic sail by shaping it like a seagull's wing. The boys would take their finished craft up to The Den Dam every New Year's Day, led by Boddam Flute Band. There they would propel their boats across the water, hoping human effort was sufficient to win. The Boddam Boys' Yachting Club decided in the 1950s to switch the races to August, too often having found the dam frozen in January and having to be broken up before the boats could sail. The ancient mine workings are still visible on the banks of The Den, perhaps the ghosts of those flint knappers puzzling at the boatie races, which continue to this day.

PETERHEAD

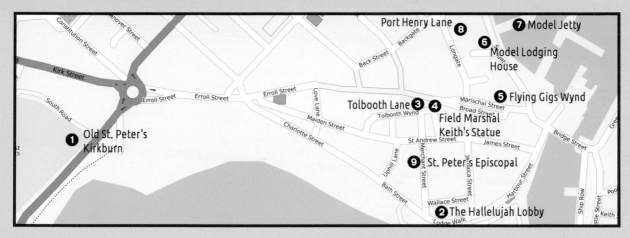

1 Old St. Peter's Kirkburn
2 The Hallelujah Lobby
3 Tolbooth Lane
4
5 Flying Gigs Wynd
6 Model Lodging House
7 Model Jetty
8 Port Henry Lane
9 St. Peter's Episcopal
   Field Marshal Keith's Statue

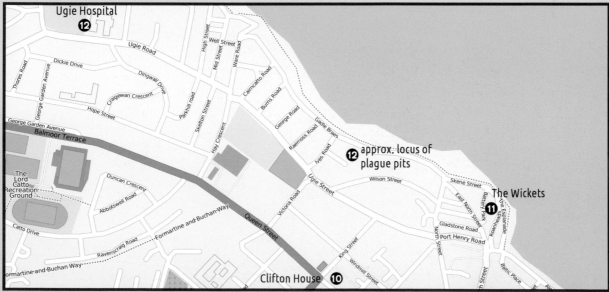

10 Clifton House
11 The Wickets
12 Ugie Hospital
12 approx. locus of plague pits

1. Six Centuries of Worship – Old St Peter's, Kirkburn

The old Kirkburn cemetery of Peterhead is dominated by its watchtower from the days of body snatchers attempting to turn a profit by supplying local anatomy schools with corpses. What is often forgotten is the solitary chancel arch, a fragment of the medieval church dedicated to St Peter dating from AD 1133. Long before the Earl Marischal ever decided to create a burgh of barony here, the local Pictish chief, Gartnait, gifted the revenue from a parcel of land called Pett-mac-Gobraig to the local abbey at what is now Old Deer. The revenue would be used 'for the consecration of a church of Christ and Peter, Apostle, both to Columcille and Drostan, free from all the exactions' on another patch of land by a stream above the natural harbour which later became the South Bay.

This was the start of the 'kirk toun' known in the old Celtic tongue as 'Pett-air-Uisge' (settlement on the water) one of three areas, which, along with Roanheads and Keith Inch, would comprise the burgh founded in 1587. The kirk was to be built 'in the Roman style', likely referring to the architecture rather than the forms of worship. The Celtic Church had developed a distinct set of beliefs and rituals, which by this time ecclesiastical leaders were trying to erase and pull into line with Rome.

In his choice of dedication, Garnait was merely reflecting local tastes: Drostan had been the local missionary to his ancestors; Columba was venerated in Scotland and Peter, the fisherman apostle, was very popular with the fisherfolk whose boats were moored in the Almanythie Creek at Roanheads. The Statistical Account of Peterhead in 1791 related that, according to Ptolemy's second-century map, the promontory on which the town was built was called Peter's Head, because of a dedication to the said Apostle. Considering the native Taezali clan were pagans, this reasoning is unlikely.

The first stone church lasted over a century before being rebuilt and extended, probably to cope with an expanding population. After the Reformation of 1560, St Peter's became Episcopalian, which although Anglican, was still Protestant. However, this was not enough for the Presbyterians who were determined that running a church with bishops and priests was theologically wrong. Did the Bible not say that there was only one way to reach God? Thus, despite most of Buchan being Episcopal, the ancient building was to host only Presbyterian services. That did not stop the Episcopalians from worshipping, as readers will discover later.

By the mid-eighteenth century, old St Peter's was way past its best. The doors were closed and the

Presbytery approved a new building which would make a grand entrance to the town. The first 'Muckle Kirk' only lasted thirty years, however, having to be demolished as unsafe in 1800. The new church was finished in 1806, complete with a bell from the famous Whitechapel founders, the same as had made Big Ben for Westminster. St Peter's was finally pulled down after six centuries as Peterhead's parish church.

2. The Hallelujah Lobby – Lodge Walk

In 1773 when James Hay, 15th Earl of Errol, commissioned the building of Peterhead's New Inn, he intended it to be a grand hotel for visitors availing themselves of the local mineral well and spa baths. Never would he have imagined it degenerating into a brothel, known locally as The Hallelujah Lobby, where famous local prostitute Lady Bell Imlah held court with her 'semi-nudist colony of voluptuous attendants'.

Mrs Abernethy, the then landlady of the New Inn, simply encouraged bad behaviour there with the founding of the 'Five Bottle Club', a sort of hellfire group consisting of local dandies solely intent on getting blazing drunk. Ultimately the well-off boozers abandoned the New Inn after the last stagecoach to Aberdeen departed in July 1861, signalling the end of Peterhead's glory days as a spa resort.

Many Peterheiders connected the name with the nearby Fishermen's Mission and Plymouth Brethren Hall, but Hallelujah Lobby was not a sacred name – far from it! Many eighteenth-century brothels had been called 'The Holy Ground', the name immortalised in an Irish folksong, but one historian believed the title originated in New York. Timothy Gilfoyle noted that from the 1770s 'in the two blocks along Church, Vesey, and Barclay streets, New York's most

Site of the New Inn

expensive "houses of debauchery" prospered on land owned by the Episcopal Church and adjacent to King's College.' The area was ironically christened 'The Holy Ground' as an attack against the church's tacit acceptance of their tenants' sinful activities. Whaling in Peterhead was at its height when Mrs Abernethy's establishment began, thus it was little surprise that the name referred to the exultation of saucy sailors as they entered the 'Hallelujah Lobby'.

The New Inn was demolished in the 1930s after decades as a private lodging house, replaced by a fine council block of Peterhead granite containing indoor plumbing. Peter 'Oxo' Buchan, the weel-kent fisher poet, had witnessed the area's transformation. He recalled meeting an old friend in the doctor's waiting room who had been a tenant of the Hallelujah Lobby in its last days. She had been advised by her doctor that she should seek better accommodation as her family's health was suffering from being confined to a few rooms in the old slum and forced to use an outside lavatory. She complained that the council could not meet the demand for new housing, and yes, there was an empty room next door, but no-one cared to live in it due to its gruesome reputation. A dark red stain on the floor had generated the horror tale that someone had been 'murdered in't lang ago'.

The doctor had accompanied her to her lodging, having secured a key from a local solicitor. Upon opening the door, sure enough, there was the bloodstain. But the doctor, fancying himself a detective, examined the stain more closely and noticed a mesh pattern. He immediately told her that she had now gained another room: this was not blood, but the place where a previous tenant had 'barked' his fishing nets. The Hallelujah Lobby 'Murder' had finally been solved!

3. George Clockie's House of Ill-Repute – Tolbooth Lane

The sight of this dark closie must have resembled a Hogarth etching in the days when George Clockie was the tenant. Neish's history of Old Peterhead paints just such a dissolute portrait: 'Tolbooth Lane witnessed many bloody fights, or some penniless, drink-besotted wretch pitched out through the door by the scruff of the neck'. So why did this infamous fellow last so long before he was finally evicted?

The Tolbooth Wynd end of the lane was once occupied by a coach house and owned by the feuars (i.e. the original rate-payers). Standing at the rear of a less dubious public house, known latterly as the Sun Inn, it was remodelled in 1805 to become a dwelling house. Mr Clockie was the first to undertake the tenancy. He probably appeared an amenable chap initially, who got on with his neighbours; his name

appears as a witness on several birth registrations for the Lawrence family who also lived in the lane.

However, it was not long before Clockie's true nature was revealed. His house became an unlicensed drinking den, or shebeen. Perhaps he was even being

supplied by the Ship Tavern, the Sun Inn's predecessor. But, wherever he got his booze, Clockie was the most popular host in town with the local volunteer militia, whose drill hall was just down the street in Smithy Close. Alcohol was not the only attraction, however, as legend states Clockie had two daughters who were very liberal with their affections.

The feuars and town managers were not above reproach for their own behaviour. Not only were they landlords of the Ship Tavern, but they regularly repaired there after council meetings for extended refreshment. Clockie had them exactly where he wanted. Eventually, after some unexplained disappearances of local soldiers, the residents of Tolbooth Lane rebelled and forced the feuars to take action. Clockie and his daughters were finally evicted and the tenancy given to one Martha Mathieson. Although it was rumoured she kept an entertainment establishment, 'Maffy' soon became famous for her boiled tripe suppers.

By 1845 the house was incorporated into the tavern buildings. Just over a century later, the fire that destroyed the town's Music Hall revealed a gruesome secret when a garden belonging to the house at its rear was dug up. Neish again is the source for this macabre tale: 'two skeletons were unearthed, with vestiges of uniform adhering to the bones!' Did George Clockie help cover up a double murder? Considering this is the only place the story appears, it could be mere fiction. However, considering the uncharitable reaction of the military to the unsolved murder of poor Lizzie Cruickshank near the Keith Inch Battery in 1812, perhaps these two soldiers were more hated than Clockie himself, thus nobody would miss them.

But today there is no trace of Tolbooth Lane, Clockie's House or the tavern. Except for an existing photograph of the Sun Inn, in which the roof of the Music Hall is evident, the whole thing might be a total fantasy.

4. Mercenary Hero – Field Marshal James Keith's Statue, Broad Street

Contained in the church of the alpine village of Hochkirch, forty miles north-east of Dresden, is a Latin memorial to a Scots nobleman. Born at Inverugie Castle in 1696, Thomas Carlyle described him as 'a man illustrious for antique character and military virtue'. He died in 1758 attempting to rally Prussian troops, of whom he was the Field Marshal, in an ambush caused entirely by the foolishness of their leader, Frederick the Great. This man, a son of Peterhead, already warned the Prussian monarch that if their enemies, the Austrians, did not take the opportunity to attack them, as they were sitting ducks, then they should be hanged. Frederick could only have taken this from no less a man than James Francis Edward Keith, named in honour of the Old Pretender; the Prussian admitted, 'We must hope they are more afraid of us than even the gallows.'

Frederick attempted to assuage his guilt after his friend and military genius died by placing a marble statue of Keith, along with other heroic generals of the Seven Years' War, on Wilhelmplatz, a prominent square in Berlin. In 1857, when a bronze copy replaced the original, Peterhead's

town council begged that they be sent the 'spare' in order to have a local memorial to their great son. But instead, William of Prussia sent them another bronze, which has pride of place in front of the old Town House, looking down Broad Street.

Few at home know of the Field Marshal's exploits, but in Germany he is still highly regarded as a military hero from a better part of their history. James Keith was, by all accounts, handsome, educated and practical. Carlyle, who met him at Frederick's court, noted Keith's 'broad accent' was 'still audible . . . through the foreign wrappages'; indeed, Keith's chosen language of communication was French, though he spoke at least six others as well as tolerable German. He only landed the fortunate position in Frederick's army because in 1747 he was forced to leave Russia after mercenary service to three rulers. The last of which was the spoilt, capricious Empress Elizabeth, who had a desperate fancy for Keith, despite the fact that he had a long-term mistress in Finnish refugee Eva Merthens. Foreigners were no longer welcome in the Russian court after the previous ruler, Anne, filled it with Germans.

Previous to this, Keith had served in the Spanish army, but ultimately found that his Protestant faith was a barrier to promotion. In Prussia, however, he found that both he and his brother, George, the 10th Earl Marischal, were most welcome. James Keith was in his forties, plagued with bad health, but was admired by friend and foe alike.

Perhaps James' greatest achievement for his family was after his death, as Frederick the Great successfully petitioned George II, Fredrick's own brother, to have them pardoned for their part in Jacobite intrigues. Forever a soldier but always a gentleman, James Keith proved time and again his family's motto, *Veritas Vincit* ('Truth Conquers'), however inconvenient for those who have to admit it.

5. Haunt of Smugglers? – Flying Gigs Wynd, Broad Street/Seagate

Flying Gigs Wynd – the very name conjures up images of dubious activities done under the cloak of night. So what is the origin of this curious little lane which began at an archway in Peterhead's Broad Street and extended around the corner to Seagate? Mr Noble, the publican of the nearby Crown Inn knew it as 'Flyingigs Wynd', but did not elaborate on its history to the Ordnance Survey researchers who recorded it in 1865. Local history expert Dr David Bertie suggests that the name was mis-transcribed from 'Flying Jib', referring to the small sail which extends beyond the boom, or horizontal mast, which carries the larger triangular sail. The lane's proximity to Port Henry and the North Harbours give some credence to this interpretation.

Dr Bertie dismisses the idea that the name referred to a horse gig, stating that the first mail coach arrived in Peterhead in 1824, nine years after a reference to the lane in Arbuthnot's *An Historical Account of Peterhead*. In the latter, the area from Flyingigs Wynd to Union Street is described as one of the original feus (parcels of land) granted in Earl Marischal George Keith's burgh charter of 1595, thus the name could be of great antiquity.

The most intriguing suggestion from oral legend is that Flying Gigs Wynd was the site of a notorious drinking den where gamblers and smugglers could enjoy illicit spirits and discuss business unmolested by the authorities. However, should excisemen, constables or – heaven forbid – the military come looking for any of these canny lads, the landlord wisely had on hand a fresh horse already harnessed to a gig so that such patrons could make a fast getaway. The origin of this story may be traced to a play written by the 'other' Peter Buchan, not the twentieth-century fisherman poet, but nineteenth-century author and antiquarian who lived at Mount Pleasant, Inverugie. *The Peterhead Smugglers of the Last Century,* penned in the 1830s, is a melodramatic love story involving William Gordon and Annie Forbes. The former is involved with smuggling, and the latter is the daughter of one Patrick Forbes, a merchant who lived in Flying Gigs Wynd. The hapless Eppy Davidson, the landlady of fictional Keith Inch Public House, describes the wares sold by Mr Forbes as 'tea and tobacco, claiths o' a' kinds and colours'.

Historically, Flying Gigs Wynd was surrounded by taverns. At the far side of Union Street lay the Black Bull and Mercat inns. Nearby Port Henry Lane had the 'Canteen', which in the eighteenth century was popular with the Redcoat dragoons and later had the reputation as another smugglers' den under landlord Andrew Chivas. The lane existed as late as 1900, as a contemporary image shows two women standing on the steps which connected the dog-leg turn to the Seagate end. By the late 1960s the Seagate exit had disappeared under Smith's ship chandlers and petrol station. The Broad Street entrance remains, yet few if any know its name or legendary origin today.

6. Peterhead's Model Lodging House – 22 Seagate

On 7 September 1896, Lord Provost John Smith of Peterhead felt justifiably pleased to announce the opening of a brand new 'model' lodging house. Situated at the corner of Crooked Lane and Seagate, it would provide accommodation for labourers, most likely those working at the harbour.

Many other towns and cities had already adopted 'modellers', as they were known, in order to improve the lives of working people. The idea was that the houses would be constructed and run to a set of agreed standards. Inmates would be taught the value of cleanliness and healthy living in order to inspire them to seek betterment. This was the Victorian self-help ethos in action: give people the education and means to improve themselves and they will not wish to return to squalor.

Two years prior to the opening of Peterhead's 'modeller', Bailie Leask and John Mitchell, who was convener of the town's Public Health Committee, had inspected some of the privately-run lodging houses. Mitchell declared that he was depressed and ashamed that Peterhead should have such dreadful places. Through Mitchell's determination; an 'energetic' committee; and the support of Provost Smith, who owned the Kirkburn textile mill, the project spawned a three-storey house of indigenous pink granite. The crowd shown around on opening day were told how it had been erected at the moderate cost of £1,500, the site itself only costing £110. With a capacity for sixty people, the lodging house offered dormitory accommodation, a communal kitchen and lounge area as well as the vital washing facilities. The male dorm had beds for twenty-eight, the female one twelve, and one floor contained six rooms for

married lodgers. The cost per night was four to six old pennies, which Mitchell explained would, even at half-occupancy, provide sufficient income to manage the house.

Local newspaper the *Buchan Observer* reported Provost Smith's comment that working people in reduced circumstances 'would find the measure of comfort and cleanliness far in excess of what they were accustomed to'. Indeed, the lodging house was designed as a temporary dwelling, where inmates would realise their lives could be far better than settling for a flea-infested doss-house. Smith said that the modeller would 'impel them to seek and obtain quiet, comfortable and respectable homes for themselves'.

From information about other modellers, we can gain a picture of what life was like. Some had a measure of privacy with partitions between each bed. For his four pennies, the lodger was given a lockable cabinet for his belongings and a tray, plate, cup and cutlery for use in the communal kitchen. Rules were strict, with a ban on alcohol, gambling and swearing. Inmates had to maintain personal hygiene and take care of the furniture. This lifestyle was for those determined to pull themselves out of abject poverty, not the layabout.

By the 1940s the lodgers had gone and the modeller had become Irvin's ironworks. Irvin's sold out in 1951 to Alexander Christie, who was succeeded by the Northern Engineering Works. Today it lies empty.

7. Model Jetty – Peterhead's Wartime Secret

All that remains of a highly secret wartime operation at Peterhead's Model Jetty is a small blue plaque located on the wall by the dry dock. The jetty was constructed from 1873 to 1878 when Port Henry Harbour, the original medieval haven, was being redeveloped to accommodate the fishing fleet. At the height of World War II, locals were hardly surprised that Norwegians had fled their occupied homeland, but no one would ever have believed they were spies gathering intelligence to aid the Allies against Nazi Germany.

Known to the Royal Navy as HMS *Sandfly*, the jetty was used by the Norwegian Secret Intelligence Service as a base from which to sail Norwegian fishing cutters and report on enemy activity in Norway. The Lyons, owners of Peterhead's Imperial Hotel, had young Scandinavian cadets billeted with them. These students were Norwegian Naval Defence Gunners, tasked with crewing the cutters. Marjorie Watt recalled that after the war her mother, Madge Lyon, was presented to King Olav of Norway, who graciously thanked her for her kindness to his subjects.

From 1941, eight boats and sixty men were involved in twenty-five to thirty successful operations, the crews as able as any of their seafaring ancestors. The Nazis were ever on the alert for spies, knowing that Peterhead and Egersund were connected by a submarine telegraph cable, which they destroyed in 1940.

The late Andy Leiper, who worked with Peterhead's Northern Engineering at the time, was, like the Lyons, sworn to secrecy as he was one of the maintenance engineers for the Norwegian craft.

He recalled the fate of *Froya*, attacked by a German bomber off Trøndelag in 1942. The crew who did not get into the lifeboat were picked up by the enemy and fiercely interrogated as to their intentions. Sticking to their story as fishermen heading for Iceland, they were made POWs. 'There is no doubt that if it had happened six months later they would have been shot. This is what happened to the crew of MTB 345.' The latter was part of the 'Shetland Bus' fleet,

aka HMS *Fox*. In 1943 the crew of uniformed naval officers – six Norwegians and one Briton – were captured after being bombed. The Nazis executed them by firing squad for being enemy saboteurs. Despite the danger, others were successful. In 1942 *Kvalsund* under Captain Einar Kristiansen journeyed from Peterhead for eight days, sailing into the Arctic Circle to deliver an agent to Kvaløya, near Tromsø, after three previous attempts had been frustrated by storms.

Another relic of HMS *Sandfly* was a bunker discovered under Peterhead's Union Bar, which closed in 2010. The pub had replaced the building in which the intelligence men used the basement as their operations room. After keeping the secret for over sixty years, Andy Leiper recorded his memories for a recent wartime project: 'It is a part of history, taking the war from Peterhead to Europe and for all the lads that lost their lives carrying it out.'

8. Home of the Jacobite Church – Port Henry Lane

'Lord Almighty, return our true prince to his throne, and raise an army in our just cause!' Reverend Alexander Barclay intones as he begins the communion service. But this Eucharist takes place not in old St Peter's, the church founded on the Kirkburn, but in an ordinary house at 3 Port Henry Lane. Reverend Barclay and his fellow Episcopalians worship in his home, after the congregation was ousted from the parish church by the Presbyterians in 1699.

So sincere is this priest in his adherence to the Episcopalian form of worship, he has already been thrown out of Turriff Church, despite trying to retain the keys when the angry locals appealed to the Presbytery. At a time when anything vaguely Catholic was feared and despised by the Church of Scotland, the Episcopal Church – still having priests and bishops – was in danger of persecution. Some, like Barclay, refused to bow to pressure to pray for Britain's new Hanoverian monarchs and retained undying loyalty to the Stuarts – hence the Scottish Episcopalians really were the 'Jacobite Church'.

Rev. Barclay seized his chance when it was rumoured that the Old Pretender, i.e. Prince James, son of the exiled James VII and II, was due to land at Peterhead in 1715. The wily priest occupied old St Peter's, Kirkburn, and prayed openly for the Old Pretender, while holding Episcopalian services in defiance of the Presbyterians. His own church deposed him for this, fearing for their precarious position, but Barclay merely returned to Port Henry Lane and continued worship in his home until his death around 1721.

Barclay's successor, Rev. Robert Kilgour, was no less fervent in his devotion to faith and monarch. His

anger was surely kindled in 1746 when Lord Ancrum, a general in the Duke of Cumberland's army, who was part of an occupying force in the town after the Jacobites were defeated at Culloden, forced Kilgour, along with his parishioners, to demolish their new chapel. Kilgour was also a resident of Port Henry Lane, and like Barclay, held services in his house until a new church was opened in Chapel Street. Conflict arose again soon after between those Episcopalians willing to pray for their Hanoverian rulers and the 'non-jurors' (i.e. those remaining loyal to the Stuarts). Kilgour and his supporters left and worshipped at a new hall in Broad Street.

The Non-Juring Episcopal Church continued to flourish despite their anti-Hanoverian stance. Kilgour was appointed Bishop of Aberdeen and later Primus of his entire denomination. In 1784, he would preside over the historic consecration of Samuel Seabury, who became the first Episcopalian bishop of the USA, an event now commemorated by an ornate memorial in St Andrew's Cathedral, Aberdeen.

Four years later, Kilgour finally decided to heal the rift between his fellow believers and agreed to pray for King George III. The Jacobite cause, like its last leader, Charles Edward Stuart, died in 1788. Today a unified Episcopal Church worships in St Peter's, Merchant Street, named after the ancient ruin on the Kirkburn.

9. A Moose Loose Aboot the Hoose –
St Peter's Episcopal Church, Merchant Street

Reverend Kilgour's Episcopal legacy in Peterhead was continued by his son-in-law, Patrick Torry. By the time Torry left his charge to become Bishop of St Andrews, the local congregation was now meeting in their fine Gothic-style church in Merchant Street, designed by local architect Robert Mitchell. Opened on Christmas Eve 1814, St Peter's, taking its name from the original church on the Kirkburn, was now the unified site of Episcopal worship in the town.

Bishop Torry was commemorated by a stained glass window installed in 1853 behind the altar; indeed the church is full of memorials to eminent members of the congregation. St Peter's is also home to two very special mice – not furry white ones, but carved oaken beasties created by the Yorkshire furniture maker Robert 'Mouseman' Thompson. The latter inherited his father's carpentry business at Kilburn in 1895, but it was not until 1919 while working on his first large commission for Ampleforth College that he carved his first rodent.

One of his workmen commented that carpenters were 'all as poor as church mice' and instantly Thompson added the little form of a mouse to the screen on which they were working. Eventually customers started requesting mice on their pieces, thus by 1930 Thompson refined the carving, removing the front legs of the mouse, which were too fragile. St Peter's mice, although having no front legs, are early examples of Thompson's wooden rodents, dating from 1926, with classic bas-relief whiskers, little eyeholes and fine whips of tails.

So who merited the large *reredos*, or rear altarpiece, on which the first mouse appears? The carved dedication on the left of the altar reveals it is a memorial to Susan Ewan Mitchell (1839–1926). Miss Mitchell was the spinster daughter of David Mitchell, mercer, ironmonger and ship owner. Her father was in business with her uncle William and whaling captain David Ewan. They established a shipping company in 1839 with the *Mary Ann Henderson*, a whaler named after William's Banffshire-born wife. *Polar Star* and *Windward*, other ships that became famous in Peterhead's whaling canon, followed. David's success would allow him to buy a grand house near Longside called Berryhill, where Susan and her sister Mary Ann lived after their father's death. Their brother William became a solicitor and then a successful tea planter in Ceylon, while his daughter, Constance, was brought up by her aunts.

Susan was highly educated in her own right, working as a foreign language teacher; thus niece Constance did not want for knowledge. The whole family were Episcopalians. William Jr, who had a house around the corner from St Peter's, was particularly noted for his generosity to the church and his fellow worshippers. William died in 1899 occasioning great sadness in the town. Susan must have continued her devotion to the church until her own death twenty-seven years later.

There is a second mouse on a shelf below the St Paul window, which was a surprise to the present incumbent, Rev. Richard O'Sullivan. Robert Thompson clearly thought that Miss Mitchell merited a bonus rodent for her unstinting service to church and education.

10. The Case of the Edinburgh Doctor – Clifton House, Queen Street

A young Edinburgh medical student with an alcoholic father from a poor Scots-Irish family is given the chance of a lifetime when a fellow medic poses the question, 'Would you care to start next week for a whaling cruise? You'll be surgeon, two pound ten a month and three shillings a ton oil money.' After being assured that his friend was offering him a job he could not take up himself, and would happily loan him his Arctic kit, Arthur Conan Doyle found his life 'deflected into a new channel'.

Indeed, it was the man who would become world famous as the creator of Sherlock Holmes and an adherent of spiritualism who turned up in Peterhead. There he sought out Captain John Gray of the town's famous whaling family and took up residency as ship's surgeon on *The Hope* in 1880.

John Gray lived at Clifton House in Queen Street. He had amassed a fortune with his three whalers, *Hope, Queen* and *Mazinthien*, and was equally successful when he and brother David invested in the *Eclipse II*, which took a staggering haul of fifteen whales and 13,000 seals in 1871.

Conan Doyle met Gray at the end of Gray's whaling career, but the fifty-year-old Blue Tooner was more than an intellectual match for the youngster. The pair would discuss literature and even resort to parodying contemporary poetry. The rest of the crew adopted Conan Doyle happily, especially after he was challenged by steward Jack Lamb to a boxing bout. Conan Doyle punched him deftly and Lamb was impressed, declaring, 'He's the best surgeon we've had! He's blackened my e'e.'

The medic was adept at hunting, but not so steady on the Arctic ice. The whalers nicknamed him 'The Great Northern Diver' after he twice fell into the freezing water but survived.

It was not all fun on the voyage, as Conan Doyle discovered, holding the body of whaler Andrew Milne as he died of an infected intestine. The wild, beautiful landscapes punctuated with the bloody work of slaughter inspired the fledgling writer in many of his future stories, such as *The Captain of the Pole Star* and the Holmes' tale *The Adventure of Black Peter.* His new-found skills as a whale and seal hunter impressed John Gray, who offered him a berth on his next trip as harpooner. Conan Doyle declined. The latter returned to Edinburgh and completed his studies.

The Gray family knew that whaling's heydays were long gone. Youngest brother Alexander shipped out to Canada to join the Hudson Bay Company, and elder sibling David took his ship *Windward* – Peterhead's last whaler – out on a final trip in 1893 before retiring to his house on the Links, now part of the Cottage Hospital. John Gray never saw that final voyage, having died the previous year. Forty winters at sea dealing with the Arctic climate had taken their toll. Captain Gray 'crossed the bar' in the same year as the first volume of Sherlock Holmes stories was published in London.

11. Through the Wickets – Roanheads, Peterhead's Original Fishertoun

'It wis aye a happy place tae bide,' Meg Bowie, former resident, told me concerning the Roanheads, Peterhead's original fisher enclave. 'Through the Wickets' was a phrase I heard often from my father, whose maternal relations lived there, and it seemed from talking to 'Roanheiders' that these gates – for indeed they were yellow level-crossing gates over the harbour spur of the Formartine & Buchan Railway – gave entry to a magical world. The extension from Peterhead's main station was opened in 1865, taking the line past the old Roanheads village, then clustered around the Almanythie, 'a small creek among the rocks where boats sometimes lie', according to Jaffray's 1759 map.

By 1875, the town's leaders had secured the right to build new houses for the fisherfolk on the old common grazing land of Roanheads Park, and four years later, five streets made up the 'new' Roanheads fishertoun. But the 'Wickets' represented the gateway between old and now. Since prehistoric times, fishermen had harvested the catches of the River Ugie and the coastal waters near Almanythie Creek, thus the 'Esplanade', as it is still called today, mushroomed into a community. Meg and her friend Jean Dickson explained that above the Wickets the boys would attach ropes to the railway footbridge which dominated the foot of Port Henry Road and swing above the rails. The girls would engage in less dangerous pursuits such as 'beddies' (hopscotch), marbles and skipping. The Wickets were their playground, as were the rocks at the creek. Margaret McLeman remembers that when she was to start her first job, she ran down to

the rocks to say goodbye, knowing her childhood was at an end.

Roanheads was self-contained: fisher widows had shops in their front rooms, supplying all their neighbours' needs. They were righteous folk who frequented the Fishermen's Mission as well as their own churches on a Sunday. Grandparents reinforced the moral education of their grandchildren. Meg's grandmother, concerned about her granddaughter's spiritual welfare, told her, 'Ye winna get Jesus in the Picter Hoose,' which she recalled again at her conversion later in life during the Billy Graham rallies of the 1960s. The men had their 'Sunday boots'; one fisherman found himself bereft when his daughters forgot to retrieve his good boots from the cobbler, so rather than don his working boots, he stayed at home that Sabbath.

Roanheads was indeed a separate world. The ladies told me that Peterhead's Queen Street had an unspoken rule that fishers kept to 'Zanré's' side and the 'toonsers' to 'Bicocchi's' side. These were cafés and ice-cream shops frequented by the local youth during the 1950s and 1960s. However, the nearby planned fishing village of Buchanhaven represented as big a threat as the townsfolk did, often resulting in fights between the 'loons' of either side.

The Wickets themselves disappeared along with the track and the bridge after 1947 when the harbour spur was closed. But to those who remember, 'Through the Wickets' represents a passage to an idyllic past of childhood freedom.

12. Beating the Bugs – Peterhead's Fever Hospitals

The Plague: believed by medieval citizens to be a divine punishment, causing them to dump the dead as far away as possible from the living to avoid spreading the disease. Around 350 people died when the Plague struck Peterhead in 1645 and wooden 'fever huts' were constructed in the area of Ive Park, a common grazing ground.

The disease was thought to have originated with the housemaid of Robert Walker. She caught it from an infected trunk of clothes sent to her from her aunt in Leith, who had just died from it. The old wooden tolbooth, situated on the Seagate, was razed to the ground, prisoners and all, for fear it too was a source of contagion.

For well over a century, the Plague pits were left fallow, the huts for the dying having been burned down and the ruins covered with earth after the disease finally passed. The feuars were keen to get their public grazing land back, thus after consulting surgeons at the Royal College in Edinburgh, the town managers agreed to return Ive Park to its former use in 1774.

Another equally hideous disease, cholera, was raging in Europe around the 1830s, and the Peterhead authorities wished to build a fever hospital and form a new Board of Health. However, the feuars were in no hurry to surrender their land again, so the scheme was shelved. In 1865, the year Asiatic cholera arrived in Britain, the town managers were finally able to purchase a two-roomed house in the fishing enclave of Roanheads in which to accommodate a fever hospital. The first permanent hospital was established in Ive Park from 1880, right on the site of the Plague pits! Locals referred to this as the 'old' fever hospital, which, like the Roanheads site, was a traditional but-and-ben-style cottage. By the turn of the century the national health authorities deemed it way below the standards for a medical facility.

It was 1904 when the town council finally approved plans by burgh surveyor T.H. Scott for a new, modern hospital specifically for infectious diseases. The chosen site was near the ancient salmon house that had been founded by Earl Marischal George Keith in 1585. There were uninterrupted views of the Ugie estuary, perhaps the reason that the building became known as the Ugie Hospital. It was completed in 1907 at a cost of £4,000 and consisted of four blocks, including administrative and observation sections. £1,500 of the cost was met by a bequest from local spinster Miss Hector. There were fourteen beds, which were pressed into service almost immediately after a severe outbreak of

typhoid made its appearance that year. Robert Neish comments in *Old Peterhead*: '[I]t was entirely due to the enlarged accommodation available for patients [. . .] that a serious epidemic was averted.'

The old fever hospital did not officially close until 1933, and was eventually demolished to make way for social housing. Ives Road, Gadle Braes and Ware Road now stand on the site of the ancient Plague pits.

CRIMOND

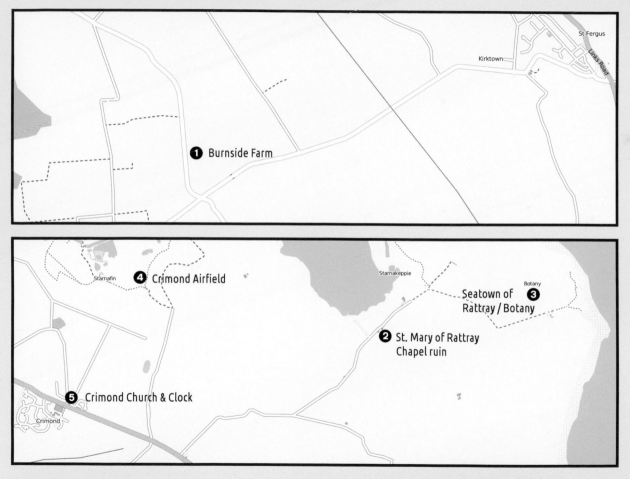

1 Burnside Farm

St Fergus

Links Road

Kirktown

4 Crimond Airfield

Starnafin

Starnakeppie

Botany

3 Seatown of Rattray / Botany

2 St. Mary of Rattray Chapel ruin

5 Crimond Church & Clock

Crimond

1. Not Proven: The St Fergus Murder Case – Burnside Farm, St Fergus

William McDonald, of Burnside Farm, St Fergus, was found dead in a ditch in a field belonging to his physician, Dr William Smith. He was lying on his back, blood issuing from a small wound on his gunpowder-blackened cheek. Surgeons later found a bullet in his brain, declaring death would have been instantaneous. This was November 1853, and suspicion lay heavily upon the good doctor, whom McDonald had told his family he was meeting on the night of his death.

Burnside Farm was situated to the west of the old village of Kirkton. It was separated from Smith's residence by a path and a field. William McDonald – a cheery lad, recently engaged, looking to purchase his own farm – was the very last person expected to commit suicide. Yet Dr Smith, on seeing the body, declared, 'He has shot himself,' pointing to the pistol which lay nearby. The outlandish statements would continue as the doctor attempted to avoid suspicion. Dr Smith later said the pistol might have gone off by accident in McDonald's pocket, which was impossible, as his pockets were too small to have contained the weapon.

Smith commented to Rev. Moir, the local Free Church minister, that there had been disagreements in the family. This was strenuously denied by them and McDonald's fiancée. When Rev. Moir asked the doctor where he had been on the Saturday night, Smith launched into a catalogue of his professional visits, giving specific times as if to suggest he was nowhere near his own house when McDonald died. Even more intriguingly, before the postmortem Smith told William's other sibling, Charles, that the deceased had

probably drowned in the water at the bottom of the ditch, as there were only 'wadding and powder' in the gun, which could not have killed him.

William Fraser, the village's bell ringer, heard the fatal shot between 7.35 and 7.40pm, and recalled 'seeing a flash in the direction of Dr Smith's field'. Miss Anderson, a patient, noted how the doctor looked closely at her clock when he arrived, which read twenty-five to eight, but she knew it was running 'a quarter slow', making his arrival time 7.50pm. Smith's servant Martha said he had been at home around 7.25pm, but had left again after ten minutes. When it was revealed in court that the doctor had three insurance policies on McDonald's life in his possession, the jury were easily persuaded Smith had planned to kill the farmer, and did so in those unaccounted minutes between leaving his house and reaching Miss Anderson's. The judge commented that this was no suicide, but an unaccountable murder to which little or no evidence connected Dr Smith. The jury took ten minutes to reach a verdict of 'Not Proven'. The foreman told the judge that it had been a majority decision between 'Not Proven' and 'Guilty'. A loud, angry hissing came from the gallery; they believed Dr Smith had killed McDonald, hoping to profit. Yet the insurers never did pay out. The St Fergus Case remained 'Not Proven'.

2. The Earl of Buchan's Chapel – St Mary of Rattray

Did a distraught nobleman commission a chapel dedicated to the Blessed Virgin, Mary of Rattray, so that prayers could be said for the soul of his drowned son? William Comyn, highest law officer in thirteenth-century Scotland and Earl of Buchan by right of his wife, Marjory, the last heiress of the indigenous Pictish rulers, had one son, Alexander, who would succeed him as earl, but also had sons from his first marriage: Walter, Richard and William. Other records mention sons David, Fergus and another William, thus it is entirely possible one of these children died in their youth and was the subject of his father's prayers.

St Mary's was a very small chapel, solely for the family's use. The walls were rubble-built and cemented with lime, giving the church a very plain exterior. The enumerators for the Ordnance Survey recorded in the late nineteenth century the discovery of a stone 'in the

eastern gable', 'marked with the date AD 1233'. Surveyors noted that the window style was typical of the late twelfth century, thus it was certainly built long before William Comyn's death in that year. He was the founder of the Cistercian Abbey at Deer in 1219, perhaps a decade after his second marriage, therefore it is more likely that William built it for his family, perhaps on an earlier site of worship used by Marjory's father, Fergus, the late Mormaer of Buchan.

Rattray itself is a puzzle. The chapel was situated near a castle, of which the archaeological remains were still being unearthed in the nineteenth century. Local farmers found silver coins in the old mound or 'motte', the artificial hill on which a wooden keep stood. John Comyn, William's grandson, had to flee Scotland and the wrath of his family's deadly enemy, Robert the Bruce, in 1308. The wooden bailey was easily destroyed by Bruce's army. John's niece, Alice, who was married to Anglo-Norman nobleman Henry Beaumont, inherited his estates. Rattray's ownership would be disputed for centuries until Mary, Queen of Scots intervened in 1563, turning Rattray into a royal burgh. This meant the tenants were subject directly to the Crown.

Had Rattray's little harbour been better situated this may have been good news, but the isthmus where the castle had stood was a mere sand dune. The north-easterly gales constantly blew the sand into the harbour, making it impossible for the fishers at Seatown to land their boats. The end came when a huge storm blocked the entrance in 1720, trapping a small boat with a cargo of slates that were 'salvaged' by the locals and used to repair roofs. The harbour, known as 'Starnakeppie', soon filled with fresh water. It is now Loch of Strathbeg nature reserve. St Mary's is a ruin, but is still associated with the Comyns. Folk have long memories in Buchan.

3. The Rattray Pirates, Fact or Fiction? – Seatown of Rattray

Alexander Harvey, the son of a West Indies millionaire, was an improving laird. When he bought the farm estate of Rattray, known as Broadlands in 1788, the British government was founding a penal colony at Botany Bay, Australia. Little did Mr Harvey imagine that his future tenants would apply this scurrilous soubriquet to the new Seatown of Rattray he created in 1795. His grandfather, a dominie in Midmar, might have warned him of the foolishness of his plan for a new fishertoun; the rocky Rattray Briggs represented the most dangerous navigable point on the whole north-east coast. Shipmasters and fishermen would repeatedly agitate for a lighthouse at Rattray Head, which did not materialise until 1895, designed by David Stevenson.

Harvey's advertisement for fishermen demonstrates his flair for spin: he proclaimed Rattray Head to be 'one of the best fishing grounds in the North of Scotland, particularly fine for cod'. The waters may indeed have abounded in fish because no sensible mariner would sail in that close to risk catching them. But the cry came too late as Charles Gordon's St Combs proved a better attraction for the majority. Four families came to Rattray from old Boatlea. They must have been very hardy souls, as their yoles could only leave the beach on the calmest of days, otherwise they would be blown into the rocks. A total of 273 vessels of all descriptions foundered at Rattray between the foundation of 'Botany' and the installation of the lighthouse. It must have been some feat of navigation to row a small sailboat past all the wreckage which accumulated there. Harvey himself was so moved by the scale of wrecks between 1800 and 1803 that he proposed a fundraising campaign for lifeboats to be stationed at Peterhead and Fraserburgh.

According to gossip, Botany fishers spent more time poaching and stealing from wrecks than actually fishing. So poor were the conditions that instead of using mussels for bait, a dead rabbit was once found in a Botany man's creel. The canny 'Rattray Pirates' would wait until the coastguard divested grounded ships of their crew, and then they would mount a 'salvage' operation. Wrecked coal boats provided a free source of fuel to the impoverished villagers. Cargoes of iron, hemp and tallow were equally useful commodities likely to generate cash if required. A spell in jail did not dent their enthusiasm, as was the case in 1870 when 'certain parties' were caught 'making free with articles from the wreck' of German clipper *Union*.

Rattray's Seatown might have attracted a criminal

element, but the stories merely highlight the ill-judged nature of the site. The new lairds, the Cumines, tried to revive Botany in the 1870s, and four fishermen duly tried their luck. By the advent of the lighthouse, the only inhabitants were the coastguards and lightkeepers. A hermit lived in one of the cottages for several years with a dog he'd rescued after finding it entangled in a barbed-wire fence. But like the 'pirates', he too passed into legend. Botany is no more.

4. How a Duck Helped the War Effort – Crimond Airfield

HMS *Merganser*, named after a rather fetching aquatic bird, was actually Crimond Airfield, commissioned 3 October 1944 by the Admiralty as a Fleet Air Arm training base. The site – now home to a popular stock-car racing circuit and the Royal Naval Wireless Telegraphy Station – is neatly slotted between belts of trees near the Crimond road and the Loch of Strathbeg.

The airfield had previously been home to Mains and Westhill Farms but from 1943, the land was commandeered by the Royal Navy and occupied by 714 Naval Air Squadron. This takeover occurred a few weeks after the devastating air raid over Aberdeen which had killed ninety-eight civilians and wiped out large swathes of the city. The men received Torpedo Bomber Reconnaissance training under Lieutenant Commander J. R. Godley, hunting down planes such as those the Japanese used to attack Pearl Harbor.

774 Squadron arrived in July 1944 to provide Telegraphist Air Gunner (TAG) training, and were later joined by 717 for the same purpose. Such units had been first introduced to the military in 1922, providing Morse communications while also manning the rear gun, a potentially deadly occupation. Four-hundred and ninety-five out of the 3,000 TAGs died throughout the branch's history.

HMS *Merganser* also hosted 753 Squadron, which arrived for Observer Training early in 1945 and remained until the following year. All units trained with the Fairey Barracuda, an all-metal British divebomber which was as ugly as its piscine namesake, and very difficult to fly. One design flaw caused leaks of hydraulic

fluid into the cockpit. The fluid's main component was ethoxyethane – better known as diethyl ether, the traditional anaesthetic – thus pilots fell unconscious and many accidental crashes occurred as a result. There were four recorded at Crimond. Sometimes Nature alone was responsible. Sub-Lieutenant Derek Allen, stationed at HMS *Merganser*, was killed along with two colleagues when his Barracuda hit Col-Bheinn in Sutherland, the hill having been obscured by mist.

The buildings remaining give some idea of the site's extent. The hangars housed the planes; the tarmac runways leading from them are still in evidence. There were fusing sheds in which munitions were 'armed'; torpedoes and their fuses were stored separately to avoid fatalities. Firing butts had the equivalent purpose of a rifle or gun range. Walk inside one and you will find a low concrete beam, which protected the trainees from ricocheting bullets. A water supply tank by a belt of trees catches only rainwater in the present, but would have been vital to operations. The control tower, rather squat by civil aviation standards, stands doorless and windowless, facing towards the runways now dominated by giant transmitter masts once operated by 81 Signals Unit at Kinloss. Sited near the airfield were two camps, Keyhead and Moss-side, where the crews were billeted during their training. Moss-side also housed a military hospital, and many of its buildings are still to be found behind Crimond Village. By September 1946, the 'duck' had flown and the airfield lay silent.

5. The Hour's Coming – Crimond Kirk and Its Curious Clock

Eagle-eyed visitors might notice something very odd about Crimond's kirk clock: between the numbers eleven and twelve, there are six strokes instead of five, giving the village its own personal time zone for one minute. The church was built in 1812 and is more famous for its association with the tune to the 'Twenty-Third Psalm', written by daughter of the manse Jessie Seymour Irvine (1836–1883). Her father, Rev. Alexander Irvine, served as the minister from 1855 to his death in 1884.

The clock originally belonged to Haddo, a seventeenth-century mansion house associated with Mains of Rattray farm estate. Haddo may have been constructed for William Watson, Bailie of Rattray, in the 1670s. Dr James Laing, owner of Haddo in the early nineteenth century, spent time abroad, as one of two British medical practitioners on the island of Dominica. His colleague, Dr James Clark, caused a furore by taking a native woman as his wife. Despite his time being spent overseas and latterly in Streatham Hill, London, where he died in 1833, James Laing was clearly interested in his Aberdeenshire property and its environs. When the old parish church of Crimond, originally built in 1576, was replaced, Dr Laing donated his curious clock.

The mechanism of the clock was regulated by a pendulum, a design invented by Dutch philosopher and mathematician Christiaan Huygens in 1657. The error lay in the clock face: it had been painted with sixty-one minutes. Dr Laing, perhaps because of his life in sunnier climes, seems to have been tickled by this and did not ask clockmakers John Moore & Sons of Clerkenwell, London, to rectify the error. We can imagine the puzzlement of the London horologists, as one of their number was sent to Haddo of Rattray to adjust the mechanism in order to cope with the odd number of minutes on the face. The clock was duly installed at the church, leaving a blank space on the mansion house's wall, which is still there today.

Zygmunt Krukowski, a Polish former soldier who had settled in the village after World War II, seemed to have comprehensive knowledge of clock workings. In 1948, he tried to repair the error by first regulating the pendulum's swing by adding old pennies as weights, and then repainting the clock face to remove the offending extra stroke. The Crimond folk were livid! They loved their curious clock and their unique time zone – what did this incomer think he was doing? Dr Laing had given them the clock with sixty-one minutes, and they would brook no argument, so poor Krukowski, thinking he had been doing his new neighbours a favour, had to undo his good works.

The black clock – with its rather apocalyptic motto 'the hour's coming' spelled out in gold text – remains in the spire, but its workings have been powered by electricity since 1994. Church elder and local councillor, the late Norman Cowie OBE, raised funds for the new mechanism. At Crimond, the hour is indeed coming, but since 1812, just a minute later than everywhere else in Buchan.

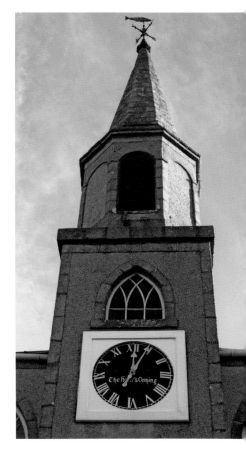

LONMAY

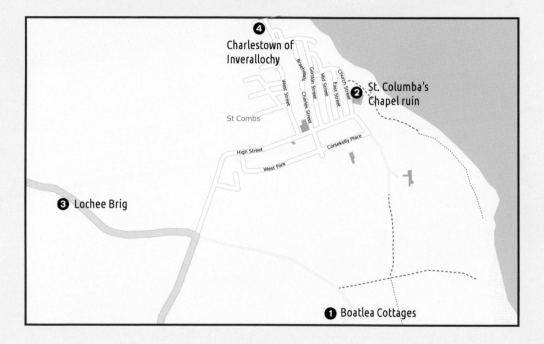

4 Charlestown of Inverallochy

Braeheads

Gordon Street

Mid Street

East Street

Church Street

West Street

Charles Street

St Combs

High Street

West Park

Corsekelly Place

2 St. Columba's Chapel ruin

3 Lochee Brig

1 Boatlea Cottages

1. Lonmay's Lost Fisher Village – Boatlea Cottages, Corsekelly

Fishing villages such as Oldcastle and Whinnyfold were curious in that they were situated high above the shoreline, forcing fishermen to lug their catch up and down steep cliffs. The fisherfolk of Boatlea were fortunate in having only mossy ground to cross to reach their fishing haven of South Cample. Perhaps the presence of the laird's gallows in the stretch of dunes between them and the beach was the real reason the fishers sited their houses so far from the shore.

For a village practically unknown today, the Seatown of Corsekelly, to quote Boatlea's official name, had ancient origins. The first mention is in the *Poll Book* of 1696, where eleven families including Buchan, Strachan, Murdoch and Mudie – names still common to the area – were listed as residing at Seatown. These were inshore 'sma-line' fishermen who employed hooked and baited lines for white fish such as haddock and cod. Their bait supply was compromised after 1720 when Rattray lost its harbour in a sandstorm, forcing them to use cockles and limpets rather than mussels. Centuries later, the farmer of Corsekelly would find buried middens full of such shells. This was the start of a slow death for Boatlea, as the locals called their village, if an odd collection of wooden cottages with their gables facing the sea could justify the term.

By 1753, the young men were desperate. Seeing no future in the makeshift haven on the sands, they went to the Kirk Session of Lonmay and begged for certificates allowing them to emigrate. The Session refused, on the grounds that the fishers should remain and support their aged parents. The estate of Lonmay was not prospering like the neighbouring ones of Inverallochy and Cairnbulg, mainly because owners the Gardens of Troup were in financial trouble. Worse still, neighbouring laird Charles Gordon of Buthlaw founded a new 'fishertoun' late in 1785. St Combs, being a planned village with a few natural harbours, was the final incentive for the restless youth of Boatlea. Twenty families moved there in 1795, the same year Francis Garden sold Lonmay to his rival. Charles' son Thomas, now the laird, invested in the new village and left Boatlea to rot.

And the floodgates opened. Once all the leases in St Combs had been taken up, the remaining fishers moved to other villages such as Roanheads and Buchanhaven. There were some who refused to budge until notices of eviction were issued. One last act of defiance came after the *Mapapima* grounded off Rattray in January 1803. When the customs men

came looking for goods missing from the ship they found them in possession of one John Cow from Seatown of Corsekelly, who was duly fined.

Oddly enough, Boatlea appears on maps long after its apparent demise, firstly in Gibb's 1858 survey and every OS Map even to the present day. Author Robert Smith discovered Boatlea Cottages still inhabited in 1991; the fishers were long gone, but the name had lived on. Boatlea was never quite lost after all.

2. Football on the Sabbath – St Columba's Kirk, St Combs

A rubble-built gable is all that is left of St Columba's, the first parish kirk of St Combs, which gave the village its name. Believed to have been founded by the Cistercian Abbey of Deer, the kirk served the parish of Lonmay from 1500. Legend states that Columba himself landed his coble at the Kirk Lakes and founded an earlier chapel, but more likely the Abbey chose the dedication since Columba was Scotland's most popular saint.

At the Reformation, St Columba's became Episcopalian, its first priest being Gilbert Chisholm, a former monk from Deer on whom James VI bestowed the charges of Lonmay, Rathen, Foveran, Peterugie and Longley (St Fergus). There was a shortage of ministers trained in the new Protestant liturgy, thus the Church of Scotland made judicious use of former Catholics who agreed to convert. Poor Rev. Chisholm was so burdened with his charges that by 1576 he was left with only Deer and Foveran. He had been succeeded at Lonmay by Alexander Barclay. The kirk began to prove too small for the numbers of fishermen and crofters who lived in the parish, thus in 1607 a new church was built inland. The minister was Thomas Rires who found that some of his parishioners were still resistant to the Protestant ways. When Rev. Rires arrived at the old kirk with his wife and family, he decided to conduct an experiment designed to endear himself to his new congregation.

Rev. Rires introduced a primitive form of football to be played on Sunday afternoons, reserved only for those who had attended the morning service. Games in kirkyards were nothing new: in pre-Reformation times, the parishioners of St Nicholas in Aberdeen allowed their children to play and even their cattle to graze around the tombs of the Mither Kirk. This decision led to tension between parishioners, not all of whom went to services on Sunday. The conflict lay in the long battle between the old Episcopalian and new Presbyterian forms of worship. The Presbyterians would do away with masses and miracles, which continually irked the people who were much attached to their old beliefs. Poor Thomas Rires' endeavour was thus a failure as the canny fishers and crofters made a mockery of his Sabbath ball games by the sea.

Rev. James Forrest, Lonmay's minister in the 1890s, wrote: '[T]he churchgoers of Lonmay do not seem to have relished their blessings for it is said they made awkward mistakes in hitting the ball whenever their toepieces could reach the minister's shins, and so put an end to the Sunday afternoon play.' Rires was probably more than relieved to move to the new church near Cairness.

The diehard Episcopalians of Lonmay eventually

built their own church in 1797, taking the name of their saint with them. The Presbyterian congregation had already outgrown their seventeenth-century kirk, having constructed a new one in 1787. This is the present Lonmay Parish Church still in use today. Old St Columba's was left to crumble. Only a stump remains overlooking the ever-changing North Sea where local fishermen still ply their trade as their ancestors did six centuries previously.

3. Murderous Intent Agin the Minister – Lochee Brig and the Mill Water

The 'Mull Waater' was the dividing line between the estates of Inverallochy and Lonmay. Today most 'New Tooners' know it as the burn which separates St Combs from Charlestown, the latter being referred to, rather uncharitably, by its neighbours as 'Soddom'. My great-great grandfather, Andrew Buchan, born at No. 11 Charlestown, was known as 'Soddam Andy' all his days.

St Combs was founded in 1795 as a planned village by Charles Gordon of Buthlaw soon after he bought the estate. Charlestown was the creation of Mrs Mackenzie, owner of Inverallochy. Perhaps envious of her new neighbour, she set up her 'fishertoun' in 1801. The biggest annoyance to the St Combs folk was perhaps that Charlestown was right beside the old mill, getting all the benefit of its supplies, including the water! The mill appears in Timothy Pont's map of the Buchan coast dated c.1580, situated on the north side of the mill burn, which flowed directly out of a large loch in front of the castle. There is a reference to a mill and mill-water in the original grant of Inverallochy estate to Jardine Comyn, the Earl of Buchan's son, in 1277, making it truly an ancient landmark.

The ford at Lochee Brig was the scene of a dramatic situation between the fishermen of Boatlea – the earlier fishing village near Corsekelly – and the new minister of Lonmay in 1709. In the century since the old kirk of St Columba had been abandoned for a new inland one, tensions between Episcopalian and Presbyterian had not improved. The Church of Scotland had banned priests and bishops, but the local folk preferred the old ways to the extent that they would do violence to unwelcome incumbents.

Rev. Thomas Gordon, a native of Aboyne, was chosen by the Presbytery since the congregation themselves had not found a replacement for John Houston, who died in 1707. The fishermen were livid; Rev. Gordon was a staunch Presbyterian. Thus they planned to do away with him as he walked by Lochee Brig on the way to his ordination. One of the wives took fright and ran to warn Rev. Gordon, who confidently told her he would come to no harm. He reached the crowd of men, armed with their lug-spades, walked up to them and told them he was so touched that they had come to meet him. 'I have heard of fisherfolk having warm hearts; to me this token of your friendship is more than I expected,' Rev. Gordon exclaimed cheerfully. The ringleader was so shocked he dropped his spade and shook the minister's hand, forgetting his murderous intent. His fellow fishers sheepishly also dropped their weapons. Instead of battering him to death, they ended up accompanying him to the ordination service and, according to one storyteller, 'remained his fast friends'.

Lochee Brig is no longer obvious, but the mill water still flows underneath the road and then appears in St Combs before reaching the sea. What had marked a division became a symbol of unity.

4. How a Priest Became Laird – Charlestown of Inverallochy

Inverallochy Castle stands as a picturesque ruin, few realising that the Mill Water connects it with the village of Charlestown, contiguous with St Combs. The former, a later addition to the coast, was first heard of when the estate proprietor, Mrs Mackenzie, advertised her resolution to 'establish a new seatown', in the *Aberdeen Journal* on 30 December 1801. It was to be named after her father, Charles Fraser, 'Auld Inverallochie', a veteran of the 1715 Jacobite Rebellion.

When the St Combs Light Railway connecting the villages to Fraserburgh opened in 1903, the estate was no longer in the hands of Mrs Martha Fraser Mackenzie, a direct descendant of Simon Fraser, 6th Lord Fraser of Lovat, whose son was the first laird of Inverallochy. Martha's last male descendant was her great-grandson, Frederick Mackenzie-Fraser, who failed to produce an heir despite two marriages. His niece, Eleanor Fraser Tomlinson, married Reverend Thomas Denman Croft, an Anglican vicar. Their son, Thomas, would later become a Catholic priest. Being Mackenzie-Fraser's last living descendant, Thomas thus inherited Inverallochy estate from his great-uncle when he was only three and took the surname Croft-Fraser.

In 1921, Thomas and his widowed mother took a holiday to Rome and never came back. The new laird of Inverallochy was admitted to the priesthood in 1927 after a period of study. He then rose to the dizzy heights of papal Privy Chamberlain and Master of Ceremonies in the Vatican. 'Don Tommaso' was known for his almost theatrical love of church ritual;

indeed, a journalist would remark that Thomas 'might have earned worldwide fame as a brilliant stage manager had he not become a priest'. Only World War II prevented him from reaching higher office, as he had to flee to Switzerland, not wishing to take Italian citizenship and therefore be an ally of Germany.

By the time Thomas's wartime exile ended, his mother had died, thus the monsignor returned to England. He worked in the Catholic Diocese of Portsmouth for some years until appointed chair of the Catholic Film Institute in 1951. Thomas's cultural interests were further indulged when he was presented with the honour of being Westminster Cathedral's Chaplain in 1955. Thomas was a gifted musician who adored Mozart, doubtless using much of the latter's sacred music in masses. Clearly he enjoyed his new post, as another Catholic columnist observed that 'there must be few priests anywhere in the world who have such an insatiable appetite for ecclesiastical functions', as Monsignor Croft-Fraser did. Indeed, even in secular life Thomas had been assistant organist at the London Oratory while working as a clerk at the Foreign Office during the Great War. He sang Vespers enthusiastically in the Vatican Basilica during his six-year term as Master of Ceremonies in Rome. The 'tall and somewhat portly grey-haired cleric' had surely inherited the Frasers' artistic tendencies, many of his ancestors having been accomplished artists. He died suddenly during an operation in November 1956, only a year into his cherished role in Westminster. His family estate was willed to the Roman Catholic Diocese of Aberdeen, who became the landlords of Inverallochy and Charlestown.

INVERCAIRN

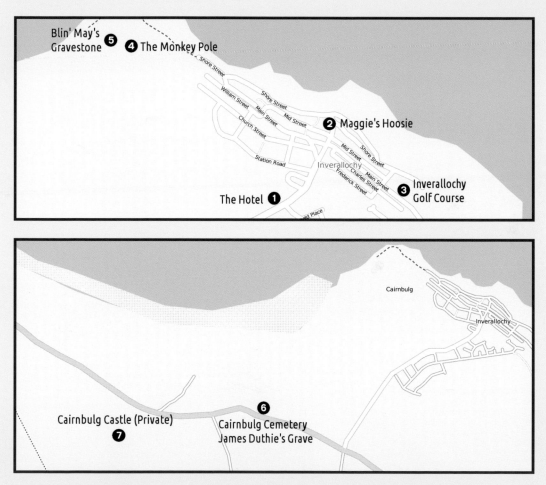

Blin' May's Gravestone ❺ ❹ The Monkey Pole

Shore Street

William Street

Main Street

Mid Street

Shore Street

Church Street

❷ Maggie's Hoosie

Station Road

Mid Street

Shore Street

Inverallochy

Main Street

Charles Street

Frederick Street

❸ Inverallochy Golf Course

The Hotel ❶

...ald Place

Cairnbulg

Inverallochy

Inverallochy

Cairnbulg Castle (Private)
❼

❻

Cairnbulg Cemetery
James Duthie's Grave

1. Voting the Parish Dry –
The Hotel, Rathen Road, Cairnbulg

The coming of the railway to the villages inspired builder William Murray to erect a Station Hotel in Cairnbulg. As a businessman he could also see his premises attracting golfers who wished to play on the Inverallochy course, but a hotel needs a bar, and therein lay the problem. The meeting of Deer District Licensing Board on 25 April 1905 became a showdown between Murray and the teetotal fishermen. Early on the Tuesday morning, the fishermen boarded the train for Maud, ready to support their legal representative, Samuel Donald, who was in possession of their 1,105-signature petition against an alcohol licence for Murray's new establishment.

Proceedings began with Murray's lawyer demonstrating that there was a desperate need for the hotel, since 'absolutely no accommodation of any kind' existed in the villages for such purposes. And there was nowhere to buy strong drink! Mr Donald spoke up and reminded him that the previous establishment, a 'small public house' had proved such a 'temptation to the young men', that the fishers banded together to buy out the property, 'causing as it did so much degradation and poverty in their midst', ridding themselves of 'what they considered was a pest amongst them'. Mr Rae mischievously suggested that the village's youth instead took the train to Fraserburgh to buy whisky and consumed it in private. Since the 1840s the Temperance Movement had been very influential in the area; the wives had been first to protest against the granting of alehouse licences in the villages, giving rise to the annual phenomenon of the Flute Band Walks. If a fisherman played in the band, he was too busy to go drinking. Provost Leask of Peterhead, a member of the board, firmly put down Mr Rae's comment, saying of the fishers 'a more sober and industrious people could not be found in the whole of Scotland'.

After Leask made a rather unfair comment against poor William Murray's 'physical fitness' to run a hotel – he had lost an eye in a quarry accident – and criticised the lack of attendance by the JPs who had signed Murray's application, he went on to complain that 'strangers' to the villages had no right to object when they did not have to experience drunken brawls on their doorstep, as had happened formerly at Mrs Carle's pub. Leask could not understand Murray's haste to have a licence, implying he did not rate his chances of success with the hotel. Chairman James Ogilvie-Forbes interjected, saying, 'What was wanted was a well-managed temperance hotel,' to which the fishermen applauded enthusiastically. Despite the

business argument, the hotel's licence was rejected six votes to two.

The hotel did operate for some years – conspicuously without a bar – even as late as 1911. Eventually it was bought by Alexander 'Sang' Ritchie, fisherman and keen golfer, and turned into a family home. It was 'an affa size o hoose', known ever after as 'the Hotel', and remains a private house today. But the fishermen got their wish – Rathen Parish had been voted dry.

2. My Ain Folk – Maggie's Hoosie, Inverallochy

The wee cottage on Shore Street, Inverallochy, has always been known as Maggie's Hoosie. The stone-flagged floor that was aye brushed clean using sand from the nearby dunes probably has not changed since it was first constructed around the 1690s. Boxed-in or recess beds feature in both the 'but' and 'ben', separated by a tiny closet where, if not occupied by the 'skull' or basket in which the fishing lines were stored, was used for a baby's cradle. In a space 8 x 18 feet wide, fisher families ate, slept and worked for generations.

Yet in 2003 I discovered an intimate connection to the hoosie: Maggie Duthie was the sister of my great-great grandmother, Annie Stephen (née Duthie). The house had been in the family from the 1820s, if not earlier. Maggie and Annie's father, Charles Duthie, known by his tee-name of 'Laudie', was the owner in the 1851 census. The girls were two of nine children. Their mother, Elizabeth (née Ritchie), was also from a fisher family, whose descendants included Evan Ritchie, who once owned the shop across the road from my maternal grandparents' house in Summerfield Place. 'Minnie', as the great matriarch was affectionately known, carried on working long after her husband's early death in 1874. In her eighties, Minnie was disabled by a bad fall while out selling fish to the local farms. She resolutely remained head of the household, despite being confined to a daybed 'at the heid o' the hoose', until her death in 1923 aged ninety-four.

Maggie's sister Annie and her husband James Stephen built their new house near the family home, but tragedy struck in 1887 when he was lost at sea, after heroically rowing his crewmates home in their tiny fishing yole in a storm. Maggie would have helped with her nephew Charles and her nieces Margaret, Jemima and Betsy, my maternal great-grandmother, as well as taking care of her own widowed mother.

By the turn of the century, Maggie still operated without electricity or running water, relying on the many 'waals' (i.e. street wells that supplied the village). She had split fish fillets drying outside, and sometimes smoked them in her own wee smokehouse. Like Minnie, Maggie went around the countryside selling fish, sometimes in exchange for dairy products, especially during the lean years of the early 1920s. She had a beautiful array of Willow Pattern plates displayed on scrubbed pine wall racks. Such treasures might have been gifts from her brothers when they visited the English ports of Great Yarmouth and Scarborough. Maggie's young relatives were always made welcome at the hoosie with the offer of 'a piece and jam'.

Maggie outlived all her siblings. In fact, when she died in 1950, 100 years had passed since her parents' marriage. She was the last of a hard-working, devout generation of fisherfolk. Thus Maggie would have laughed to think the hoosie had now become a museum when it was simply a fisherwife's home.

3. Putting Like a Demon – Inverallochy Golfers vs the Parliamentarians

A century is a long time to wait for revenge, but in 2003, the golfers of Inverallochy had a score to settle with the Parliamentarians of Westminster. In April 1905, just before the licensing board debacle, Alexander 'Sang' Ritchie and teammate Robert Stephen teed off against Prime Minister Arthur Balfour and Eric Hambro, member for Wimbledon, at Royal St George's in Sandwich, Kent, scoring a resounding 2–0 victory. This, however, proved too much for the English gentlemen to stomach, thus they hammered the fishermen 11–2 by the end of the day. The Inverallochy team, previously undefeated in Scotland, returned with pride severely dented.

The trip had been organised by MP for East Aberdeenshire Alexander Maconochie, who owned food-processing factories in both Aberdeen and London. For the Scots it was a nice wee holiday, and the team became celebrities as they toured the sights of London including Buckingham Palace, St Paul's and the House of Commons, where one Cottoner commented he 'didna ken fit they were sayin, but it's somethin' aboot the Transvaal'. Standard English may have been an issue, but not world affairs, as local newspaper the *Fraserburgh Herald* had a regular column for global news. According to the Broch correspondent, the weather on match day was 'of the most delightful order,' and after Sang's early win, the Cottoners soon lost any nerves they might have had. It would seem the Parliamentarians exploited the teetotal Scots over lunch by plying them with wine, a trick that did not work in the return match in 2003. No wonder the journalist could say, '[A] happier gathering of golfers I never saw.'

Fast forward to the fundraising match in the present century when the MPs team led by House of Commons Speaker Michael Martin turn up to the course, first founded in 1888. Alex Salmond, still Banff & Buchan member at the time, was reckoned to be a secret weapon, having had a low handicap as a student. Yet it was Tavish Scott, in his unpopular post of Finance Minister, who dazzled the attendant press pack with his playing. Journalists described him 'putting like a demon' off a handicap of ten, completing the first nine holes one stroke above par thirty-four. The Shetlander, though used to sea breezes which waft across Inverallochy's seaside links, couldn't repeat the success of Arthur Balfour and his Tory chums back in 1905. Vengeance was sweet for the locals; a 'total whitewash' ensured that the honour of the fisher-golfers – of which many had come from the Ritchie family – was restored.

Andy Buchan Tait recalls how talented Sang's Alex, the son, was with a particular type of golf club 'he used tae scunner me wi' his cash-in putter[1], so deadly!' Three generations of Ritchies proved to be excellent players. As Andy puts it, '[T]hey made up the backbone of the Inverallochy Abercrombie Cup team, which they won on more than one occasion. All very nice to play with but deadly serious when it came to the crunch.'

[1] *a golf club specifically for putting, with an extra-long grip*

4. Monkeys Never Climbed This Pole – Cairnbulg Rocket Apparatus

The curious wooden structure encased in an iron support stands approximately 100 yards from Cairnbulg's harbour, overlooking the former coastguard station. It was a vital part of the life-saving practice drill for the 'Rocket Brigade', the volunteer force who represented the RNLI in the Fraserburgh area. The 'rocket pole' represented the mast of a ship at which the volunteers would fire a thin rope propelled by a rocket, while another man sat atop the pole waiting to catch the rope.

Once the rope was fired, it allowed a larger rope and the breeches' buoy to be attached to a stricken ship off the coast. The rocket-powered version was invented by Cornish civil engineer Henry Trengrouse in 1808. He had improved on the earlier mortar-powered line designed by eccentric Norfolk inventor Captain George Manby. Both proved popular with the Admiralty and were a boon to the RNLI, formed in 1824. Fraserburgh Lifeboat Station introduced the rocket apparatus to several nearby fishing villages in 1826; both the pole and 'apparatus house' appear on maps of Cairnbulg Harbour area from this period onwards. Improvements were made in succeeding years, principally by John Dennett in the Isle of Wight. The most recent rocket was designed for the Board of Trade by Colonel Edward Boxer, Superintendent of the Royal Laboratory at Woolwich. Col. Boxer is also famous for designing the friction tubes for Edinburgh Castle's famous One o'Clock Gun.

Belger locals remember the 'monkey pole' with great affection. Andy Buchan Tait recalls, '[T]here aye wis a scramble for the match fan my Didie eesed tae fling it doon efter lichtin' the rocket.' One practice session resulted in a broken rope and the rocket flew far across the fields, ending up on the main road to Fraserburgh, right outside the Cairnbulg cemetery!

The Wick-registered fishing smack *Rose* ran aground at Fraserburgh Sands in January 1827. Its crew of three men, two women and a child were rescued by breeches' buoy after the coastguard 'with the assistance of several ship masters, promptly brought Capt. Manby's apparatus to the spot, and succeeded in firing a warp across the vessel'. Lifeboat skipper Lieutenant C. H. Bowen, a naval officer, was given a gold medal and the coastguard crew were given monetary awards for their part in the rescue.

In March 1881, the Cairnbulg apparatus itself was used to rescue the crew of the German barque *Friedrich Perthes*. The Bremen-based ship had been heading for Granton in Midlothian, bearing a cargo of jute; however, having already made the long journey from the USA, heavy seas forced her onto the rocks of Inverallochy bay. Sadly, one man was lost.

As of 2007, Fraserburgh had a brand new lifeboat station, and at the time of writing it has a Trent-class lifeboat, *Willie and May Gall*, which has had ten call-outs since June 2013. Cairnbulg's life-saving apparatus was last used in 1985. The coastguard station is now a private house and the monkey pole a mere curiosity of a bygone age.

5. Blin' May's Grave – Cairnbulg Harbour

Near the monkey pole there is a muckle stane which my mother remembers as a child being warned by her cousin not to jump on because it was 'some wifie's grave'. Indeed, at one time, according to Johnny May of Inverallochy, the stone bore the name 'May', but due to the kindness of two women in Cairnbulg, there is now a cast-iron marker that tells May's story.

Her name was Marjory Mowat, but she was known as 'Blin' Mah'ee', or Blin' May. Her death during the cholera epidemic which struck the village in 1849 is tragic enough, but the fact her remains lie under the grassy dunes not far from the harbour tells us something about the awful nature of the disease. Johnny again takes up the story, 'Before Belger had a cemetery, folk were buried at St Combs kirkyard. The toon folk wouldn't let her be carried through the villages with the fear of . . . getting unwell, so she was buried here.' According to her simple memorial, Blin' May was between eighty-six and eighty-nine years old when she died.

Characterised by sickness, diarrhoea and profuse sweating, cholera

first appeared in Britain in 1831. Careless officials in Sunderland allowed a Baltic ship to dock and the epidemic resulted in 52,000 deaths across the country. This particular outbreak began in 1848. Information from the minutes of Fraserburgh's Police Commission reveals that in October 1849 'householders be warned under the pains of the law, not to receive into their houses individuals from the infected district'. Cairnbulg fishermen returning from Montrose were the carriers. They arrived on 30 September with the body of their crewmate who had already succumbed. The father of another crew member was infected as he helped them unload. His family died within days. A report by health inspectors observed that the next victim had attended one of their funerals. The cholera swept like wildfire through both Inverallochy and Cairnbulg, taking fifty lives. Inspector Grieve attributed the rapid progress to primitive sanitary conditions: 'Water in stagnant pools. Dunghills near doors, consisting of fish refuse with seaweed and dirty water from the houses.' Grieve noted too that the disease had passed between the villages via the Stripey, the stream which flowed down a shallow gully dividing the main street. The water had been infected by contaminated clothes being washed therein.

So why was May Mowat treated thus? The real issue was the fact that St Combs kirkyard was in the neighbouring parish of Lonmay; the residents managed to persuade Peterhead's Sheriff Substitute to issue an interdict banning any burials there unless carried out by the parish gravedigger, precluding any of May's relatives from doing so. Rather than risk infection by waiting, the Belger emergency committee decided to inter the body in that lonely spot near the harbour, likely causing unspeakable grief to her surviving daughters. Blin' May's grave thus represents an act of fearful haste at a time of crisis, yet it ensured she would never be forgotten by succeeding generations.

6. Dummy Jim: The Man Who Cycled into the Arctic Circle – Cairnbulg Cemetery

It was 1951 and James Duthie's thirtieth birthday gift to himself was a cycle tour which would take him on a 10,000-mile round trip from his native Cairnbulg to Sweden's Arctic region. Deaf since childhood, 'Dummy Jim', as he was known, communicated by sign language. He showed his neighbours a map and indicated he was heading for Morocco. The Belgers knew James loved his bike; he had already been to Austria and Switzerland on previous tours, so this latest trip was no great surprise.

James possessed a great deal of historical knowledge about every country he saw, as is evident in the little prose sketches he provides along the journey in his book, *I Cycled into the Arctic Circle*. He was also an artist, we read, when James recognises his own painting on a friend's wall in Denmark. How did a deaf man travel with such apparent ease? The deaf community had their own network, primarily through schools all across Europe. James had attended Donaldson's College in Edinburgh, and the journey gave him the opportunity to meet former classmates and connect with other deaf of many nationalities. When James writes about having grand conversations, a casual observer would only have seen silent individuals with highly animated hands. The deaf world is full of words, pictures, smells, tastes, and knowledge, which hearing people imagine they are denied.

James made a quick decision to abandon his route to North Africa after replacing a worn screw on his bike courtesy of an 'old French engineer in Gonesse.' He explains, 'I feel it may last a long run on a long

JAMES DUTHIE
AUTHOR
1921 – 1965
"I CYCLED INTO THE
ARCTIC CIRCLE"
AND HIS MOTHER
ELIZABETH DUTHIE
1882 – 1936

route,' and suddenly he was off to Belgium where he found he 'could buy plenty of sweets' there without any ration coupons.

I followed James' route on a map as I read. He covered a phenomenal amount of ground but makes it sound like a simple trundle round Cairnbulg. At Stockholm's deaf school he simply announced he would 'attempt to cycle to the North Cape', the Arctic region of Sweden. When the schoolmaster tried to dissuade him, James tells us, 'I see he is a person of no courage.' A few pages later, James is in Kiruna, Sweden's most northerly town, communicating with the native Laplanders. Although he found it too lonely and dangerous to reach the North Cape, James was soon on his way back to Belger, reaching home by August the same year.

This fascinating man would complete an even longer journey of 14,000 miles in the 1960s, but he only published one book. Silence eventually claimed James Duthie when he was killed near Stracathro after a motorbike accident in 1965. Almost fifty years later, film director Matt Hulse was given a copy of James' book and decided to bring his adventure to the cinema. James would 'speak' again through the hands of deaf actor Samuel Dore, who bears a strong resemblance to the late James Duthie, the man who cycled into the Arctic Circle.

7. Home to Roost – The Frasers and Cairnbulg Castle, Philorth

Cairnbulg Castle, once the Manor House of Philorth, was originally home to the Comyn family. Their keep was one of the 'nine castles of the Knuckle', a coastal defence system to protect against the threat from Viking invaders. Once Robert the Bruce became king of Scots, he tried hard to wipe out his royal rivals who could claim direct descent from Donald Bán, brother of Malcolm III, both grandsons of Malcolm II, the Celtic king who defeated the Danes in AD 1012. The barony of Kinnaird in which Philorth Manor stood was granted to Robert's Lord Chamberlain, Alexander Fraser of Cowie, who was the second husband of the king's widowed sister Mary Bruce. Alexander's grandson married the heiress of Ross, bringing with her the lands of Buchan and restoration of the castle's original tower c.1375.

So Cairnbulg Castle mushroomed over the centuries into the present family home consisting of five parts, occupied by the Honourable Mrs Katharine Nicolson since 1997. On a recent visit, she told me that a group of local schoolchildren studying the castle for their lessons were disappointed she was not wearing a ball gown and a tiara. 'It would be rather difficult to do the hoovering in a tiara,' Mrs Nicolson commented. It is indeed a family home, with pet dogs, rows of shoes at the back door, and ordinary cars parked in the driveway, and until recently it was the home of the chief of Clan Fraser, Mrs Nicolson's mother, Flora Fraser, Lady Saltoun. Her father, Alexander, 19th Lord Saltoun, had bought back the castle in 1934 after generations of displacement due to their ancestor, the 8th laird, having to sell it in 1613 to pay the debts incurred by founding Fraserburgh and its harbour. Previous owner Sir John Duthie, the Aberdeen shipbuilder, had restored the castle following years of neglect.

Old castles contain secrets. Just as the Wine Tower may have held the 8th Lady Fraser's Catholic chapel, Cairnbulg has some old heraldic panels that could refer to a troubling conflict between the Saltouns and the Lovats. Mrs Nicolson showed me the marriage lintel stone belonging to Alexander Fraser, 12th Lord Saltoun and his wife, Mary Gordon of Haddo. The coat of arms bears the ostrich crest, a symbol borrowed for the town's arms, which also appears as the three-dimensional bird atop the municipal fountain outside Bellslea Park. A near-identical marriage stone sits beside it, but the bride's heraldry has been erased. Both Lady Saltoun and her daughter agree that this may have been the panel to celebrate the proposed marriage of Alexander and Amelia Fraser, heiress of

the 9th Lord Lovat. The engagement was cancelled after Alexander's father was threatened with the gallows by Amelia's cousin Simon Fraser and uncle Thomas, who kidnapped Saltoun on his way to make the final arrangements for the wedding.

These days old rivalries are forgotten and the Frasers are back in the home their ancestor Alexander of Philorth built with his wife, Joanna Ross, over six centuries ago.

FRASERBURGH

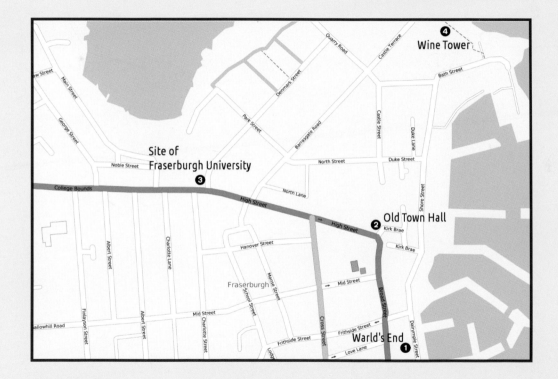

Site of
Fraserburgh University ❸

Wine Tower ❹

Old Town Hall ❷

Warld's End ❶

Fraserburgh

1. Old Glenbucket, Jacobite Rebel – Warld's End, Dalrymple Street

Warld's End – a curious name for a site mentioned as early as 1650. The property now bearing the name is a two-storey stone building with central roof pediment and an external staircase. Sandwiched between the Dalrymple Hall and the Caley Fisheries offices, Warld's End was restored to its eighteenth-century glory in 1980 by architect Herbert West. The only reason it is here at all is down to one man's fanaticism for the Jacobite cause. John Gordon, laird of Glenbuchat and bailie to the Duke of Gordon, might have had the tiniest estate in Strathdon, but he left a reputation that far outweighed his earthly possessions.

Born in 1673 on the Glenbuchat estate, bought by his father from other Gordon cousins, John seems to have been steeped in loyalty to the Stuart family from the beginning. At sixteen he fought in John Graham of Claverhouse's army at Killiecrankie and this set the course of his life for the future. At forty-two he led a regiment in the 1715 Jacobite Rebellion, but after defeat at Sheriffmuir, he surrendered to his enemies. This action probably saved his neck.

Under the cover of loyalty to George II, Glenbucket* meanwhile plotted to raise the standard again for the Old Pretender, James Francis Stuart. By 1738, he sold his estate to William Duff, Lord Braco, and bought a farmhouse in Tomintoul and the site for a townhouse in Fraserburgh. The latter purchase made sense since his nearest neighbour was the arch-Jacobite Alexander Forbes, Lord Pitsligo. The remaining funds Glenbucket used to finance a trip to Rome to persuade Cardinal Fleury, the French king's chief minister, to mount a Franco-Scots invasion to seize back the

British throne. The parsimonious Cardinal said, 'Non!'

However, Old Glenbucket, now in his sixties, rallied several prominent Scots Jacobites including the Duke of Perth, the Earl of Traquair and Simon Fraser, Lord Lovat, all of whom were willing to start another rebellion. If Glenbucket was an inveterate Jacobite, he was also a ruthless leader, as many of the young men he recruited would later testify. He press-ganged teenage boys into the Jacobite Army, sometimes carrying them off in bonds. It is almost unsurprising that Culloden resulted in massive failure with an army of poorly trained, poorly equipped boys and old men.

Despite Glenbucket's belief in the cause, he was forced to play hide-and-seek with his Hanoverian pursuers after the battle. His heavy-handed treatment of his tenants made them only too willing to betray him. Glenbucket scurried around Aberdeenshire like a hunted fox. He eventually escaped to Norway, heading to Boulogne in France where he died amongst a group

of disillusioned exiles. World's End was attainted along with Glenbucket's other possessions, and auctioned in 1766. In the twentieth century it was owned by John Findlayson, who ran the Dalrymple Hall and Café.

Yet, despite dying in ignominy and poverty, the old Jacobite haunted George II to the last; the German king would often wake up screaming, 'Der great Glenbucket is coming!'

* John Gordon was latterly known as 'Old Glenbucket', from an archaic spelling of the estate name.

2. The Hielandmen's Riot – Old Town Hall, Saltoun Square

Fraserburgh's old Town Hall on Saltoun Square housed the court, the police station and a market. Twenty-one years after it was built, a group of alcohol-crazed Highland fishermen battered down the door and threatened to raze it to the ground. It was August 1874, the fishers' payday, and the Highlanders went on a pub crawl. Around midnight, John Buchanan, a large, burly 'wild Celt', resisted arrest and then punched Sergeant Grant of Fraserburgh Constabulary. Buchanan was diverted to his lodgings in Back Street, where all hell broke loose on the stairs of the house. The police intervened again, resorting 'to free use of their batons', as the *Aberdeen Journal* later reported.

The Highlanders then got the idea that Buchanan had been taken to the cells, thus they surged towards Saltoun Square. The three constables who had been at the lodging house pursued them, only to discover their colleagues were besieged in the police office. Around 300 to 400 hundred men were gathered outside, throwing stones at the windows, smashing both glass and frames, determined to effect the rescue of their pal. The language barrier did not help; only one constable, MacPherson, spoke Gaelic, and despite his pleas in their own tongue, they would not be moved.

Next, a sturdy wooden spur was procured and the mob used it as a battering ram, 'before which the door soon gave way'. From the cells the Highlanders heard the roars of fellow fisherman Walter Grant, who had been arrested earlier in the evening. They attempted to free him, as well as destroying any property they could get their hands on. Meanwhile, the constabulary cowered upstairs, utterly outnumbered. Inspector Richardson tried to tell the mob that Buchanan was not there, but Grant would be released if they removed themselves. The Highlanders replied they would burn the place down if Buchanan was not found. The local militia had got wind of the incident and were advancing towards the Town Hall armed

with carbines. It was only due to the command of Major Ross, the Chief Constable of Aberdeenshire, who happened to be in town, that the militia did not fire. A summer downpour also helped to disperse the crowd, who had held the town in terror for two hours.

But the angry Celts sent word to their fellow fishers at other ports to form a greater army, thus next day

Major Ross brought in fifty soldiers from the Gordon Highlanders' Regiment in Aberdeen to protect the town from further nuisance. The soldiers accompanied the constables as they searched the boats for the ringleaders, apparently by examining heads for particular wounds! Three men were arrested. Ewen McKay from Sutherland and James Innes – a local carter who had joined in the rioting – were both later jailed for twelve and nine months. John Buchanan skipped bail and was declared an outlaw by Lord Ardmillan. Even fifty years later, in my grandfather's lifetime, the story of the night the 'wild Celts' had the Broch Bobbies at their mercy was a well-known legend.

3. The Broch's University – College Bounds/Denmark Street

Old Aberdeen and Fraserburgh share the street name College Bounds, but the only college in the Aberdeenshire town is Banff & Buchan College, situated in Henderson Road. What *did* happen to the University of Fraserburgh? Apart from the street name, the university's only surviving relic is the Moses Stone, a stone sculpture depicting Moses receiving the Ten Commandments, which is now on display in the South Church, Seaforth Street. The church, completed in 1880, replaced the old parish school where the Moses Stone was displayed above the main door. According to Rev. Simpson, author of the 1793 Statistical Account for Fraserburgh, there was 'an old rectangular tower of three stories, a small part of a large building intended for a college', at the junction of College Bounds and Denmark Street. The site is confirmed by the 1869 Ordnance Survey map.

James VI granted local laird Alexander Fraser of Saltoun the funds to start a university and the Privy Council approved the project in 1594, making it the first academic institution in Scotland not founded by the Pope. In 1597, an Edinburgh minister, Charles Ferme or Fairholme, was invited to become principal and take up the charge of Philorth. Along with Crimond, Tyrie and Rattray, the parish would provide the income to run the new university. Considering Fraser himself was an Episcopalian and his wife a Catholic, it is strange indeed that he should have chosen Ferme, who turned out to be a staunch Presbyterian, unafraid of protesting against government action which favoured Catholics. However, for the first few years, it would seem that Principal Ferme got on with establishing

Fraserburgh University in its purpose-built premises.

Two years after James VI became king of England, and thus a united 'kingdom', this wily monarch decided to impose his authority on the Church of Scotland. The latter made it quite clear that Christ was their sole head, but James suspended the meeting of ministers at the 1605 General Assembly without giving any hope of them being allowed to reconvene. Nineteen ministers defied the king and held their assembly. James, livid at such behaviour, not only sent a messenger-at-arms to disperse them, he jailed eight of their number, Ferme being one of them. After imprisonment in Doune Castle, the thirty-nine-year-old minister escaped, vowing that the Privy Council had no spiritual authority over him. Ferme was eventually caught in 1607 and incarcerated, latterly on the Isle of Bute. Alexander Fraser ensured he was still paid his stipend that year, but finding himself in financial straits after spending so much on his new burgh, he could

not support his beleaguered principal in 1608.

Ferme was released in 1609 and restored to his ministerial charge. He returned to Fraserburgh, enjoying his salary and stipend for the remaining period until his death eight years later. King James had learned that the Church of Scotland would not be manipulated by an earthly monarch. Fraserburgh University, however, never recovered its reputation and disappeared without a trace. The kirk had won the day, but principles cost the Broch its first and only principal.

4. The Lady Vanishes –
The Wine Tower, Fraserburgh Lighthouse

Farewell, earth's all of good / Our bridal waits below the tide, were the reputed final words of Isabel Fraser, daughter of Alexander, 8th laird of Philorth and founder of Fraserburgh. As the story goes, the lady's lover, a poor piper, had been imprisoned by Isabel's father in the Selchie's Hole below the Wine Tower, which was part of the laird's coastal estate at Kinnaird Head. He had drowned when the tide flooded the extensive cave, and Isabel wept for grief when she saw him. She seized his dead body and jumped from the roof of the tower. Where she fell, the lighthouse keepers painted the rocks red in memoriam.

This really is a fairytale, as although Alexander Fraser had three daughters, none were named Isabel, but were married to three local noblemen, Cheyne of Esslemont, Hay of Ury and Keith of Inverugie. Far from being a tyrant, Alexander was an improver. He was given charters from James VI in 1588 and 1592, one allowing him to create a 'free port'* at Faithlie harbour, and the other confirming the burgh of barony given by Mary, Queen of Scots in 1546.

Kinnaird Castle thus became the Frasers' home, built around 1570 along with the curious tower. Ostensibly a wine cellar, speculation has raged for years as to its original purpose. Lady Flora, the current chief of Clan Fraser, believed it to be a hidey-hole for the laird and his buddies to carouse without interference from their womenfolk. Historian Ian Bryce stated that, 'The entire structure was designed to prevent the viewing of its interior', suggesting the activities therein were to remain secret.

It is now well established that the top storey

was fitted out as a Catholic chapel for Alexander's wife, Magdalen Ogilvie. In the immediate aftermath of the Reformation, many Catholics worshipped in secret, and Lady Fraser was no exception. As an Episcopalian, Alexander would have happily accommodated her faith; indeed, he did so to such an extent as to allow the 'Arma Christi' to be displayed in the chapel's vaulted ceiling. This was a symbol which depicted Christ's hands, feet and heart pierced with the five wounds received on the Cross, popularised by a Catholic sect focused on the Easter Passion. The fact that the only entrance was from the middle storey, originally reached by a ladder, made the Tower an ideal sanctuary for religious purposes. Perhaps Magdalen's brother, Walter Ogilvie, a priest, even visited and said mass with her in private.

By 1786 Kinnaird Castle was sold and turned into a lighthouse, leaving the Wine Tower to be used as a store. In 1803 and the 1860s it held a gunpowder magazine when all Britain feared invasion by Napoleon's forces. St Margaret's Chapel, Edinburgh, similar in shape to the tower, also housed gunpowder for the local garrison until 1875.

Today, there is still a dramatic splash of red painted on the rocks; ghostly pipes are said to play on stormy nights. Perhaps Isabel Fraser's existence was wiped from written history, but oral tradition has allowed her tragic story to persist.

* i.e., free of taxes and dues to locals using the harbour, just as a medieval royal burgh protected the rights of local traders and merchants.

ABERDOUR

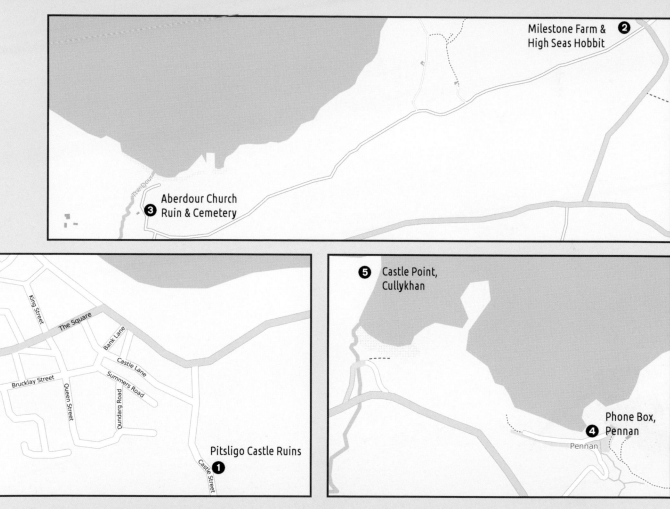

Milestone Farm &
High Seas Hobbit ❷

Aberdour Church ❸
Ruin & Cemetery

The Dour

Pitsligo Castle Ruins ❶

Ward Road
King Street
The Square
Bank Lane
Castle Lane
Summers Road
Brucklay Street
Queen Street
Dundarg Road
Castle Street

❺ **Castle Point,**
Cullykhan

Phone Box, ❹
Pennan

Pennan

1. The Jacobite Who Was Never Caught – Pitsligo Castle, Rosehearty

Though the storm rages overhead, the cave is strangely silent and warm. *Like the belly of the whale in which Jonah languished*, thinks Sanny. As the wind blows itself out, the old, ragged, wheezing beggar moves from his hiding place and makes the journey over the fields to Rosehearty. Above the fishertoun are the castle and its fine gardens, which he can just discern through the twilight. He ambles down the farm track by the ancient stone and knocks at the door of the kitchen. A young maid answers it, sees the aged beggar, but then, looking more closely, realises his kindly eyes are very familiar. She beckons him inside then races to her mistress's room. 'Mistress Forbes, it is His Lordship!' she cries.

This is no fantasy. The old man was Alexander Forbes, Lord Forbes of Pitsligo; his disguise as 'Sanny Broon', the holy beggar, was adopted after the disaster of Culloden in which his tenants and friends lost their lives and his Prince finally lost the throne of Britain for the Stuarts.

Alexander was the fourth Lord Pitsligo, an Episcopalian and a lifelong Jacobite, or supporter of the Stuart dynasty. He was known as a beneficent landlord and a devout Christian. 'Out' in the 1715 Rebellion for the Old Pretender, Pitsligo had to flee to France to avoid arrest after the campaign's failure.

Having escaped serious censure, Alexander returned to Pitsligo Castle and tried to lead a peaceful life. But his support for the Stuarts drew him back into conflict by 1745. In his sixties and asthmatic, Pitsligo was an unlikely figure in Bonnie Prince Charlie's army, but he was treated with great respect by the latter. A contemporary likened Pitsligo's venerable presence to 'religion, virtue and justice entering the camp'.

Yet the Prince, despite so many wise military veterans in his army, made a foolish choice of battleground at Drumossie Moor, and the rest was indeed history. Pitsligo had enough. He dressed as a wandering mendicant, or religious beggar, and made his way home to Buchan. He remained in this disguise for the rest of his life, but latterly lived with his son at Auchiries House near Memsie.

Many are the stories of how 'dressed in his rags' he tricked the government troops (Redcoats). Pitsligo's tenants were well aware of the disguise, often pleased to entertain him in their humble dwellings. He almost fell foul of the Redcoats while visiting a local shoemaker's shop. The latter told Pitsligo to don a workman's apron and wield some tools. As the soldiers observed the work, the shoemaker feared that the sight of his lordship's soft hands would betray him, so he sent him to attend to a horse out of their view. It was thereafter humorously said that Pitsligo was 'a Buchan cobbler'.

Alexander Forbes died at his son's house in 1762, having finally regained his estate from a forgiving Crown. Yet wisely, John Forbes did not advertise his father's funeral: the locals just knew Sanny Broon had passed away aged eighty-five.

2. Hobbits in the Shire – Milestone Farm, Rosehearty

No, they are not Tolkien's hairy-footed creations now re-popularised by film director Peter Jackson, but two tubular wooden lodges representing the recent trend for 'glamping' (i.e. glamorous camping). Complete with fridge, microwave and electric light, the High Seas Hobbit, constructed from loglap timber on the outside and antique satin pine inside, first appeared on the Aberdeenshire farm when owners Carole and Matthew Short needed something to supplement their agricultural income.

Carole wanted to provide holiday accommodation, but something small-scale with a unique twist. Enter Steve Millar from Fife, inventor of the original 'hobbit' microlodge, which first evolved from a quick drawing on a wall to a serious suggestion for a new type of accommodation at a campsite in Crail. Having previously built the microlodges for campsites and hostels in Kinlochleven, Glencoe, Tyndrum and even as far afield as County Wicklow, Ireland, it was a simple matter for Steve and business partner Gary to deliver the first 'hobbit' to Rosehearty in 2012.

Steve explained how the hobbits had changed since the early days: 'We now fit high-end double-glazed doors and windows, have increased the overall size of the units, fitted hardwired smoke alarms, installed carbon monoxide alarms, and we are always looking for ways to improve.' Using local timber suppliers and sustainable insulation – recycled plastic bottles – Steve found that the microlodge's simple but eye-catching design complemented the natural surroundings 'unlike a big white caravan that leaps out at the eye'.

Back in Rosehearty, 'glampers' have exclusive use of a field that overlooks the sea and is kitted out with

a firepit. Carole commented that most customers love the outdoor fire and starry night skies in which the Aurora Borealis occasionally makes an appearance. The last glampers of 2013 'arrived with fireworks, food, fleeces and most importantly, fantastic smiles upon their faces,' wrote Carole on High Seas Hobbit's Facebook page. The family in question duly replied that they had had a great time.

When I went to visit on a blustery December day, it was quiet and cosy inside the microlodge. The first thing Carole did was switch on the kettle. Having camped the traditional way, I was delighted with the warmth and innovation in this twenty-first-century form of holidaying. Like me, many others have discovered the hobbit through social media: customers have come from America, South Africa, Germany, and even Kazakhstan.

The site even has a shower block and a toilet facility so innovative it recently won the Loo of the Year Award. Carole and Matthew collected their award from TV doctor/presenter Hilary Jones at a ceremony in Solihull. The outdoor 'watery', is closeted in a massive whisky barrel a few strides from the larger of the two microlodges.

The couple are both from farming backgrounds, but Matthew hails from Bath. He explained that his family moved to Aberdeenshire over twenty years ago when the Somerset countryside was becoming utterly congested with smallholdings. Now with sheep, cows and two hobbits, the Short family are enjoying their role as local exponents of agri-tourism.

3. The Unwelcome Incumbent – St Drostan's Church, Aberdour

1733: Britain is ruled by a Protestant monarch and Scotland's official religion is Protestantism. However, this made little difference to those of the Catholic and Episcopalian faiths in Aberdeenshire. Ostensibly Protestant since the 1560 Reformation, the Parish of Aberdour contained many who remained loyal to Episcopacy. The sixteenth-century church, today in ruins, was first dedicated to St Drostan, a sixth-century Irish missionary who, along with fellow monks Machar and Colm, established Christianity among the local Celtic tribes.

From the Restoration of the monarchy in 1660, Rev. William Ramsay had been ejected as an unwelcome Protestant and replaced by Alexander Reynold, an Episcopalian. The latter was ousted after William of Orange's coronation in 1689. The locals made life as difficult as possible for the next incumbent, John White, who was not even officially inducted as minister. Despite his attempts to be faithful, his temper apparently got the better of him, as we learn he was 'deposed for cursing' in 1694. His replacement, Rev. James Brown, who arrived in 1697, fared better, remaining until 1733, when he became minister of Longside.

Several prominent local Protestants were determined to overturn Episcopacy and its stranglehold on Scotland's religious life once and for all. As a result, the Protestant Rev. James Turing was inducted as minister on 21 September of that year. Turing came not only from a family of ministers – his father and uncle incumbents at Drumblade and Rayne respectively – but also from noble stock. His elder brother, Alexander Turing, was Baronet of Foveran. The family could trace their origin to William de Turin, who was given the title by David II of Scotland in exchange for his military successes. However, thirty-one-year-old James, who had been educated at King's College, experienced the ire of the locals as soon as he arrived. His ordination was refused by the Presbytery of Deer, the ruling ecclesiastical court for the churches in that area. But his noble friends persisted and appealed to the next level of church government, the Synod, who ordained James Turing 'by commission'.

Twenty-nine days later, he was found suspended by a rope from a beam in the manse; James Turing had taken his own life. Incredibly, the incident was quickly and conveniently forgotten by Deer Presbytery, who inducted Rathen-born Thomas Anderson the following year. However, historian John B. Pratt commented in 1858: '[T]he circumstances of five individuals having died violent deaths within the space of as many years, was sufficient, in the popular mind, to fix the crime upon them.' Rather than charge Turing with the sin of self-slaughter, ordinary folk preferred to believe he had been driven to his death by the men who opposed him. The tragic irony is that in 1954, James Turing's descendant, the mathematical genius and wartime code-breaker Alan Turing, would also die by his own hand. Many believed that he had been driven to it by those who disapproved of his lifestyle. It is unimaginable the stress that led these two intelligent men to commit suicide, yet the name of Turing is not forgotten in Aberdeenshire – Alan's nephew is the 12th Baronet of Foveran.

4. That's Show Business –
Pennan and Its Famous Phone Box

Scottish filmgoers in 1983 might just remember the delight of seeing 'kennt' places in *Local Hero*, the BAFTA-winning story of a US oil man's attempt to buy a tiny fishing village. Pennan starred as the fictional hamlet of Ferness, and the village's red phone box also made an appearance. Movie buffs visiting thereafter have rushed to get their 'selfies' alongside this symbol of British film history. However, just as the beach in the film is not in Pennan, but in Mallaig, that communications edifice didn't actually exist there either! Prop designers made a phone box and placed it in the middle of the shore for cinematic convenience, removing it afterwards. The Pennan folk were furious: if film fans were going to come calling, they would expect a phone box! British Telecom answered their plea and installed a working one, turning it into a piece of cinema iconography; hence it gained listed status in 1989.

But what attracted director Bill Forsyth to this remote spot where Pennan and its neighbours, Crovie and Gamrie, nestle on the coast like seabirds? The village's history seems to date from around the time the first harbour was built in 1704. The 'Fish Town' was first documented on cartographer James Robertson's 1822 map of Buchan. Pennan farm is recorded in 1696 as belonging to James Baird, the 6th laird of Auchmedden. His ancestor, Andrew Baird, had moved to settle at Auchmedden in 1534 from Fife, where he had owned the coastal village of Elie – thus the foundation of a 'fishertoun' would have been nothing new for him. This line of Bairds died out in 1750, Auchmedden, and thus Pennan, being sold on

to Lord Aberdeen (i.e. Gordon of Haddo House). Their new laird saw fit to replace the crumbling pier and harbour in 1799.

The Bairds returned to Auchmedden in 1834, but this family were rich industrialists from Lanarkshire, who did not reign long. Their line extinguished by 1893 with the feckless George Baird, a millionaire playboy who died of pneumonia in a New York hotel after a drinking binge. Auchmedden ended up in the hands of a speculator who broke up the estate by selling off all the separate elements. George's only obvious contribution to Pennan was part-funding a Chapel of Ease* in 1884; Auchmedden Church still stands above the village today.

Were the folk of the village anything like the film? One Alexander Watt, born 1878, gave his occupations as 'shoemaker, salmon-fisher, post-master' on his marriage to Mary West in 1900. This adaptable fellow may well have been the inspiration for actor Denis Lawson's character George Urquhart, who seems to run every institution in Ferness. There was even a real hermit who, unlike the film's Ben Knox, did not own a beach, but lived in a cave near Aberdour Beach. Known simply as Jock, he was an eccentric retired sea captain called David Reid, who died in 1936. Unlike that iconic phone box, these folk certainly did exist in this windswept settlement, which has clung limpet-like to the sandstone cliffs for more than three centuries.

A Chapel of Ease was an additional church built in a large parish where not all the congregation lived near enough to the main church to attend.

5. Aberdeenshire's Forgotten Forts – Castle Point, Cullykhan

Nobody knows what the Iron Age (c.700 BC–AD 500) peoples of Scotland called themselves, but Roman geographer Ptolemy attempted to categorise them into separate tribes, of which the Taezali inhabited most of Aberdeenshire, their capital being Devanah, cognisant with Aberdeen. One of their major coastal defences was sited at Cullykhan. The latter, Ptolemy believed, marked the border between them and the Vacomagi. In more recent times this was the border between Aberdeenshire and Banffshire, a long tree-lined ravine through which the Troup Burn flowed into the sea.

Cullykhan Bay encompasses the promontory known as Castle Point, upon which the Taezali built a wooden fort strengthened by stone ramparts. But since the 1960s, excavations have revealed the promontory was in use since the late Bronze Age, around 3,000 years ago. Digging down below the location of the fort, evidenced by post holes and vitrified rock, the team from Aberdeen College led by archaeologist J.C. Greig found a layer of industrial waste in the shattered remains of a crucible. The introduction of metalworking to Stone Age farmers must have seemed like alchemy, as the liquid mixture that forms bronze – copper and tin – was poured into a mould then beaten into implements of a quality far superior to their flint and granite. Examples of chisels from c. 1,000 BC suggested the gradual dominance of iron over bronze as the essential construction metal for weapons and tools.

The forts came after ordinary occupation, as did many Roman finds, weaving a tale of defence against

the enemy from the south, just as the Comyns would do centuries later on this coast to repel the Vikings using stone castles armed with cannons. Two more phases of fortification showed the addition of stone ramparts and a large impressive gate. Doubtless the Celts had seen the Roman palisades built above protective lines of trenches and borrowed their ideas.

The same Taezali would attempt to cast the Romans out of Buchan in the battle of Mons Graupius c.83AD when they engaged them near either Bennachie, where three Roman camps were located, or the camp of Raedykes, Stonehaven. The Romans were the victors, but the Celts who survived disappeared into the hills, where the trained warriors knew it was unwise to follow. Pot sherds dating between AD 300 and 400 also found at Cullykhan showed that such forts continued to be ideal hiding places while the Roman presence remained in Britain. But even after the Romans withdrew, Cullykhan remained a strategically

important site. In the thirteenth century, the Troup family built a keep described as 'a Norman tower house'. The Barony of Troup passed to the Keiths until the 1690s, when it was purchased by the Garden family. Out of the abandoned tower they created a coastal battery, known as Fort Fiddes, which lasted just over a century. Now only grassy outlines remain on this, one of Buchan's most strategic promontories.

Cullykhan represents the end of this journey along Aberdeenshire's historic coast, reminding the intrepid explorer that history is indeed under our feet and on our doorstep.

Acknowledgements

Massive thanks to the following: All my friends who shared stories personally or through social media, including Johnny May, Andy Buchan Tait and Jenny Smith for information on Cairnbulg's 'Hotel', the golfing prowess of the Ritchie family, Blin' May and the Monkey Pole. The members of various Facebook groups who provided suggestions and ideas *(Fisher Folk of Scotland, St Combs Lang Syne, Inverallochy/ Cairnbulg Then and Now).* My good friend Pauline Cordiner for allowing me to use the words of her late father, George Cordiner, concerning the Boddam Monkey. Marna Cruickshank for her invaluable knowledge about Cruden Bay and the Episcopal Church of St James the Lesser. Margaret Garfit (neé McLeman), Meg Bowie and Jean Dixon for the wonderful reminiscence session on 'the Wickets' and Roanheads. Mrs Heather Lawson for allowing me to use the words of her late father, Andy Leiper, concerning the wartime naval base at the Model Jetty. The Honourable Mrs Katharine Nicolson of Cairnbulg Castle, for her hospitality and tour of her family home. Film director Matt Hulse for his insights into the story of 'Dummy Jim'. Jim McDonald, retired police inspector, for his insight and useful leads into the history of the Broch riot. Pre-history expert Mark Keighley for his pointers on Cullykhan and The Den Dam. Carole and Matthew Short of High Seas Hobbit for letting me visit their microlodges and to inventor Steve Millar for providing background information on the microlodge's origin. Ack and Marlene Cowie for making me so welcome at Crimond Kirk; Ainsley and Ian Dyga of Fraserburgh for putting me in touch with them. Rev. Richard O'Sullivan for showing me the Mouseman carvings at St Peter's, and Chris Scaife, archivist and historian, for Robert Thompson Ltd., for his information on the church mice. The staff of Peterhead and Fraserburgh Public Libraries for their help in locating books and information on various aspects of this manuscript. The biggest thank you of all goes to my parents: my mum for her proofing and editing skills and my dad for remembering things about Peterhead long ago.

Glossary

Belger	A native of Cairnbulg. Although only separated by a narrow stream, Cairnbulg and Inverallochy were rivals in the sense that they belonged to separate landlords.
Blue Tooners	A nickname for inhabitants of Peterhead. Being the most north-easterly point in Scotland, it is always blue with cold!
Broch, The	A nickname for the town of Fraserburgh, from the old word for a fortress, perhaps referring to Kinnaird Castle, which became the lighthouse.
Buchan	The traditional name of the land before it was called Aberdeenshire. It has origins in the Celtic words for cattle pasture. Legend has it that Edward Bruce, brother of Robert, told the Earl of Buchan's family that their lives would be spared if they dropped the name Comyn and adopted the surname Buchan instead.
conchoidal fracture	Geological term for a crack creating a rippled pattern similar to that on a conch shell, hence 'conch-oidal'.
Cottoner	A native of Inverallochy. The town is known as Cotton for two possible reasons: one is that being originally part of an agricultural estate, it was a 'Cott-Toun'; another is that on the land where the golf course now stands hemp and cotton were grown in ancient times.

'*Cuir críoch na Dane*'	Gaelic phrase meaning, 'Kill the Danes', or literally, 'Make dead the Danes'. My understanding of where historians got '*Croij Dane*' from.
crossing the bar	A maritime expression for death, after Alfred, Lord Tennyson's poem of the same name.
Drumossie Moor	The site of Culloden, the final battle in the 1745 Jacobite Rebellion, which took place 16 April 1746.
Earl Marischal	A hereditary office of the Keith family since the twelfth century. The Great Marischal was the monarch's bodyguard at court and custodian of the royal regalia. William Keith was made Earl c.1458 by James II of Scotland.
Episcopalian	A form of church government involving bishops and priests, used by both the Catholic and Anglican Churches.
Egyptian campaigns	World War I campaign fought by the Allies against the Turks, who supported the German forces of the Kaiser. Led by the Egyptian Expeditionary Force, originally under the command of General Archibald Murray, and later General Edmund Allenby. The latter asked James McBey to be their official war artist. T.E. Lawrence was able to inspire the Arabs to fight for the Allied cause, but was angry when there was no further aid to give the Arabs their own independent state.

Faithlie	The old name of the settlement out of which Alexander Fraser created Fraserburgh, his burgh of barony. The name was used recently as the name of the Ice Company at Fraserburgh harbour.
feuar	The original tenants of the burgh of barony created by Earl Marischal George Keith. The feus were portions of land offered in return for an initial investment and further annual rent/rates. The feuar-managers thus formed the first 'town council' of Peterhead.
Fishermen's Mission	The Royal National Mission to Deep Sea Fishermen, a Christian charity founded to aid seamen physically and spiritually by Ebenezer Mather in 1881
GNSR	Abbreviation for Great North of Scotland Railway. The Buchan & Formartine line that served most of Aberdeenshire was part of GNSR.
Invercairn	Shorthand for the twin villages of Inverallochy and Cairnbulg.
knapper	One who shapes and works flint into tools and weapons; 'knapping' is the act of working flint.
kerb cairn	A burial cairn featuring a mound of small diameter that is surrounded by a kerb of stones considerably taller than the mound. These date to the early Neolithic period (4000 – 3000 BC).

Monsignor	The honorific title given to officers of the Catholic Church by the Pope granted to those who have rendered valuable service to the Church or who provide some special function in church governance. Thomas Croft-Fraser, being both Papal Privy Chamberlain and Vatican Master of Ceremonies, was addressed as Monsignor.
Mormaer	Gaelic, meaning 'Great Sheriff', equivalent to an earl in Celtic times. Mormaers were minor kings of their areas of Alba, that is, early Scotland. The Mormaer of Moray was Macbeth's father, Findleach MacRuraraidh.
Motte-and-bailey	The motte was a man-made earth mound surmounted by a keep, usually built of wood, occasionally of stone. Introduced to Britain by the Normans in the eleventh century and widely adopted by native noblemen and the Norman settlers. The bailey was a separate linked enclosure for ancillary buildings.
New Toon	As St Combs is known by locals of nearby villages. Since it was a planned village, rather than an organic one, this probably explains why it was called the 'new toon'.
North of Scotland Bank	The building that housed this bank was designed by Archibald Simpson, Aberdeen's most famous architect, in 1838 and stood on the corner of King Street and Castlegate. It later became the Clydesdale Bank and is now a pub.

Old Pretender	One of the less flattering titles given to James Francis Edward Stuart, son of the deposed James II of Great Britain. James' sister and her Dutch Protestant husband, William, were accepted as the new monarchs when their father's open Catholicism terrified the Protestant leaders. Also known as Chevalier St George, and by Jacobites, his supporters, *James III*, a title that was never his. Father of Charles Edward Stuart, the Young Pretender, Bonnie Prince Charlie.
Presbyterian	A form of Christian church government utilising a series of courts from kirk session, presbytery and synod up to General Assembly. Used by the Protestant Church of Scotland after the Reformation of 1560, which outlawed Catholicism.
Rattray	Former royal burgh once owned by the Earls of Buchan. The name could translate as 'Rath-Traigh', Fort on the Beach or 'Rath-Reidh', Fort by the Harbour. Local pronunciation is *Rottra* or *Rattra*.
River Ugie	Peterhead's main river. It is twenty-one miles long and has its source in Windyheads, Aberdour. The main tributary is the South Ugie Water. Perhaps the inspiration for the original township's Celtic name, *Pett-air-Usige*, 'settlement upon the water'.

Roanheads	One of the earliest fisher settlements in Peterhead, sited by the natural haven at Almanhythie, which translates as 'Old Man's Hithe'. Further expanded from the 1870s using the old common lands of Roanheads Park.
Sodom	A nickname for Charleston of Inverallochy, a planned village founded by Martha MacKenzie-Fraser c.1803, across the Mill Water from St Combs. Nicknamed by inhabitants of the latter due to the increased pressure they would put on the resources in the area.
'The Tinkers' Wedding'	A tune associated with the popular folk song 'The Day We Went to Rothesay-O'.

Bibliography

Aitken, Margaret. *Six Buchan Villages*. Peterhead, Scotland: *Buchan Observer*, c.1976.

—. *Six Buchan Villages Re-visited*. Dalkeith, Scotland: Scottish Cultural Press, 2004.

Arbuthnot, James. *An Historical Account of Peterhead from the Earliest Period to the Present Time*. Aberdeen, Scotland: D. Chalmers & Co., 1815.

Bertie, Dr David. *Scottish Episcopal Clergy 1689–2000*. London: T.&T. Clark, 2000.

Bruce, Stanley. *Fraserburgh Through the Years: An Illustrated History of the Broch*. Banff, Scotland: Bard Books, 2010.

Buchan, Peter. *The Peterhead Smugglers of the Last Century, or, William and Annie, an Original Melodrama in Three Acts*. Edinburgh, Scotland: Thomas Stevenson, 1834.

Coull, Sam. *Nothing But My Sword: The Life of Field Marshal James Francis Edward Keith*. Edinburgh, Scotland: Birlinn, 2000.

Cranna, John. *Fraserburgh: Past and Present*. Aberdeen, Scotland: Rosemount Press, 1914.

Directory to Noblemen and Gentlemen's Seats, Villages etc in Scotland. Edinburgh, Scotland: Sutherland & Knox, 1857.

Ferguson, David M. *Shipwrecks of North East Scotland, 1444–1990*. Aberdeen, Scotland: Aberdeen University Press, 1991.

Gilfoyle, Timothy J. *City of Eros: New York City, Prostitution and the Commercialization of Sex, 1790–1920*. New York, New York: W.W. Norton & Company, 1994.

McKean, Charles. *Banff & Buchan: An Illustrated Architectural Guide*. Architectural Guides to Scotland Series. Edinburgh, Scotland: Mainstream Publishing, 1990.

McLeod, Rev. N. K. *The Churches of Buchan and Notes by the Way*. Aberdeen/Edinburgh: A.&R. Milne and John Menzies & Co., 1899.

Neish, Robert. *Old Peterhead*. Peterhead, Scotland: P. Scrogie, 1950.

Scott, Hew. *Fasti Ecclesiae Scoticanae: The Succession of Ministers in the Church of Scotland from the Reformation*. Vol. 6. New Edition. Synods of Aberdeen and of Moray. Edinburgh, Scotland: Oliver & Boyd, 1926.

Shepherd, Ian. *Aberdeen and North-East Scotland*. 2nd ed. Edinburgh, Scotland: HMSO, 1996.

Smith, Alexander. *A New History of Aberdeenshire, Part 1*. Edinburgh, Scotland: Blackwood, 1875.

Smith, Robert. *One Foot in the Sea*. Edinburgh, Scotland: John Donald, 1991.

Summers, David W. *Fishing Off the Knuckle – the Fishing Villages of Buchan*. Aberdeen: Centre for Scottish Studies, University of Aberdeen, 1988.

Tocher, James F., ed. *The Book of Buchan*. Peterhead, Scotland: The Buchan Field Club, 1910.

Online Sources:

Clan Fraser website. Authored by Lady Saltoun, chief of the name and arms of Fraser: http://www.fraserchief.co.uk/

Dummy Jim film website by director Matt Hulse: http://dummyjim.com/

The Modern Antiquarian. Authored by Julian Cope. Site dealing mainly with archaeological and prehistoric sites: http://www.themodernantiquarian.com/home/

National Library of Scotland Maps Collection: http://maps.nls.uk/

Royal Commission on the Ancient and Historical Monuments of Scotland (RCAHMS): http://www.rcahms.gov.uk/

The Statistical Accounts of Scotland 1791–1845. Hosted by the Universities of Glasgow and Edinburgh: http://stat-acc-scot.edina.ac.uk/

The Workhouse: The Story of an Institution: http://www.workhouses.org.uk/

QUESTIONING HISTORY

The Cold War

Sean Sheehan

HODDER
Wayland

an imprint of Hodder Children's Books

© 2003 White-Thomson Publishing Ltd

Produced for Hodder Wayland by
White-Thomson Publishing Ltd
2/3 St Andrew's Place
Lewes BN7 1UP

Other titles in this series:

The African-American Slave Trade
The Causes of World War II
The Holocaust
The Western Front

Editor: Anna Lee
Designer: Jamie Asher
Consultant: Scott Lucas
Picture research: Shelley Noronha,
Glass Onion Pictures
Proofreader: Philippa Smith

Published in Great Britain in 2003 by Hodder
Wayland, an imprint of Hodder Children's Books

British Library Cataloguing in Publication Data
Sheehan, Sean, 1951-
   The Cold War. - (Questioning history)
   1. Cold War - Juvenile literature
   I. Title II. Lee, Anna
   909.8'25

ISBN 0 7502 4085 7

Printed in Hong Kong, China

Hodder Children's Books
A division of Hodder Headline Limited
338 Euston Road, London NW1 3BH

Picture acknowledgements:
AKG 32; Camera Press 14, 21, 22, 30, 41, 43, 45,
46, 52; Corbis 10; HWPL 4; Impact 53; Mary
Evans 9; Novosti title page 47, 49, 54; Peter
Newark's Military Pictures 5, 7, 8, 18, 19, 29, 33,
40; Popperfoto 15, 25, 26, 35, 39, 51, 56, 57, 58;
Topham cover, 16, 36, 37, 48, 50.

The maps on pages 11 and 13 were created by
Nick Hawken. The maps on pages 20, 24 and 28
were created by The Map Studio.

Cover picture: 19-year-old Conrad Schumann
reported for duty as an East German border
guard on August 15 1961. When the other guards
had turned their backs, the young soldier made his
break to the west to join his family which had fled
earlier.

CONTENTS

CHAPTER 1

Who Started the Cold War?

The Cold War is the name given to the period from 1945 to 1991 when a high level of distrust existed between two superpowers, the USA (also called the US) and the USSR (also called the Soviet Union). The Cold War dominated world events because each of the two superpowers tried to influence the world in ways that suited its own interests. These interests were based on very different ideas about the organization of society, which led to each side fearing the other.

BELOW *Leaders of the USSR, USA and Britain meet for the last time at the Potsdam Conference in July 1945. Their agreement to divide a defeated Germany into different zones of occupation would, unknowingly, prepare the ground for the outbreak of the Cold War.*

GLOBAL CONFLICT

The Cold War also led to a series of conflicts in different parts of the world where the two superpowers found themselves in confrontation. In some of these situations, the state of mutual fear led to a dangerous level of tension because each superpower possessed many nuclear weapons. However, despite some close calls, the conflict never developed into a

state of direct armed war between the USA and the USSR. Such a direct war would have been a 'hot' war and, because this never happened, the opposition of the USA and the USSR continued to be called the Cold War.

The Cold War lasted for some 45 years and over the course of this time it involved conflicts in more parts of the world than World War II. In Central and South America, in Africa and the Middle East, and in central and South-east Asia, real wars caused by the Cold War led to the deaths of millions of people. The course of world events was shaped by the Cold War and, even after it had ended, the consequences continued to influence events in different parts of the world.

ABOVE *Each side in the Cold War regarded its own economic and social system as superior to the other. This cartoon is an example of how the USSR saw the economic systems of the USA and Britain, with ordinary workers as the victims of capitalism.*

? WHAT IF...

there was a World War III?

There were moments during the Cold War when there was a very real risk that one of the superpowers would launch an attack on the other side, using nuclear weapons. It is very likely that this would have brought a counter-attack, unleashing more nuclear weapons. The countries of Europe, as allies of one or other of the two superpowers, would have been involved, and possibly other regions of the world. The result could have been World War III. What if this had happened? Given that the USA and the USSR had enough weapons to destroy the world, and all life on it, several times over, World War III would have threatened the survival of civilization as we know it.

THE COLD WAR STARTS

On 25 April 1945, American soldiers crossed the Elbe River in Germany to meet with Russian soldiers from the Union of Soviet Socialist Republics (USSR). They hugged each other in joy and danced together to celebrate their joint victory over Nazi Germany. The armies of both countries had fought their separate ways across Germany. The Americans came from the west after landing in northern France on D-Day, and the Soviet army came from the east after beating back Hitler's invasion of their country. Now they had come together in a symbolic moment that represented the defeat of Nazism and the end of World War II.

? EVENT IN QUESTION

The Cold War: whose history?

As with any historical event, there are various aspects to the Cold War over which historians do not agree. However, in the case of recent conflicts such as the Cold War, the different opinions held by historians may be affected by the fact that they grew up during the period in question. The following points are worth considering when reading about the Cold War.

• Who is writing? It is worth looking at any information provided about the author's background and experience. Even professional historians interpret aspects of the Cold War in different ways and an account by an American, say, could be quite different from an account by a Russian.
• When was it written? Was it written during the Cold War, when perhaps it was more difficult to step back and view what happened as a part of history? If it was written after the mid-1990s, the author may have had access to information that wasn't previously available.

The political leaders of the Allies had met during the war to discuss their common aim of defeating Germany. On 17 July 1945, they came together for their last war conference amidst the ruins of Berlin, Germany's capital city, but there was no hugging or dancing. Despite having supported each other during the war against a common enemy, there had been an earlier history of mistrust and this now began to make itself felt once again. The deep mistrust went back to the consequences of a revolution in Russia in 1917 that led to a Communist government and, later, the creation of the USSR. This Communist government abolished private property and claimed it would build a new society based on ideas of social and economic equality for all.

ABOVE *Comrades-in-arms. Soviet and American soldiers first met on the 25 April at Torgau on the River Elbe in Germany. Two days later, when this photograph was taken, they repeated their first joyful meeting for the cameras.*

7

COMMUNISM AND THE WEST

The idea of communism frightened countries such as Britain and the USA, whose rulers thought the 1917 Russian revolution might lead to similar revolutions in their own countries. After the 1917 revolution, they had invaded Russia and unsuccessfully tried to depose the new government. It was 1933 before the USA established diplomatic relations with the Soviet Union, and the alliance between the two countries during World War II was more a matter of convenience than anything else. The USA transported tanks and other aid to Russia in order to help defeat Germany. Yet despite this, the USSR remained suspicious of the USA and Britain, feeling they should have made their D-Day

RIGHT *This poster from World War II, showing the Union Jack, the Stars and Stripes and the Hammer and Sickle in the foreground, celebrates the fact that Britain, the US, the USSR and other nations were allies fighting on the same side.*

landing in Western Europe at least a year earlier. The Soviet Union felt, with some justification, that it had been left alone to withstand the Nazi war machine.

ABOVE *Soviet troops drive past the Austrian parliament building in Vienna on their way to western Germany in April 1945.*

THE SUPERPOWERS

The national wealth of the USA was greater after the war than at any stage before. The country produced over half of the world's total manufactured goods and owned two-thirds of the world's gold. The USSR also emerged in the post-war world as a superpower. Despite having lost some 27 million citizens in defeating Germany, the Soviet Union possessed a powerful, undefeated and huge army. It was now determined to make sure that never again would its land be invaded from the west. As its army moved across Europe towards Berlin, attempts were made to set up governments that would be friendly towards the USSR (see map on page 15).

? PEOPLE IN QUESTION

Joseph Stalin (1879-1953)

Joseph Stalin became ruler of the USSR in 1924 and in 1945 he was determined to keep the Soviet Union safe from the threat of any future invasion. He made it clear that neighbouring countries such as Poland would not be allowed to have governments unless they were firm allies of the Soviet Union. The USA was not trusted and the Marshall Plan (see page 12) was seen as an excuse for America to extend its economic power. The West did not understand Stalin's preoccupation with the future security of his country. According to some historians, the aggressive attitude of the USSR towards building a firm defence against the West contributed to the beginning of the Cold War.

POST-WAR EUROPE

Britain emerged from the war as a virtually bankrupt country, dependent on financial support from the USA, which now wielded the global power once held by Britain. The defeated nations of Japan and Germany were in a state of economic and political collapse. In 1945 Germany was divided between the Allies in what was planned as a temporary measure until a non-Nazi government could be formed. The city of Berlin, which lay in the eastern half of the country, was also divided between the Allies. Meanwhile, France and Italy, both very weak and in need of economic assistance, had popular communist parties that looked to the USSR as their model. There was no dominant power in Europe and if communist parties were elected to government in France and Italy they would be friendly towards the USSR.

BELOW *Cities like Berlin, shown here in 1946, had to be literally rebuilt after World War II.*

This situation alarmed the USA because America was keen to promote its idea of freedom, which meant an economic system built on private enterprise and the right of people to travel freely. Soviet society was based on the idea that the common good was more important than freedom of the individual, and the country's wealth was owned by the government. These differences resulted in the USSR becoming preoccupied by a need to protect itself against any future threat to its security from Western Europe. The situation in defeated Germany after 1945 meant that the USA and the USSR were on a collision course, driven by their different priorities.

ABOVE *After the Second World War, Germany was divided into areas occupied by the USSR, Britain, the US and France. The inset map shows the three air corridors between Berlin and the West.*

? PEOPLE IN QUESTION

Harry S. Truman (1884–1972)

Harry Truman became President of the United States in April 1945 and it was soon made clear that his administration would adopt a hard-line attitude towards the USSR. Truman was convinced by the arguments of many of his advisers who said that the Soviet Union could not be trusted and that it would try to expand its power and threaten the American way of life. Truman declared there was a clash of values between 'alternative ways of life' and that the Soviet Union needed to be contained. This aggressive attitude, which became known as the Truman Doctrine, has been seen by some historians as contributing to the development of the Cold War.

Who was Responsible for the Cold War?

Historians do not agree over who started the Cold War, though many see both the USA and the USSR as being responsible in different ways. The beginning of the Cold War was like a game of ping pong, with each side responding to a move made by its opponent. One of the first moves occurred when the USA decided to strengthen the economies of countries in Western Europe and win their support with the Marshall Plan. Named after the then US Secretary of State, George Marshall, and announced in 1947, this scheme devoted huge amounts of money to dealing with the food shortage and lack of industrial production in Europe. Six months later, a new American government organization, called the Central Intelligence Agency (CIA), secretly channelled millions of dollars to opposition parties in Italy to prevent a communist party winning a general election that took place there in 1948.

The USSR became even more suspicious of the USA when details of the Marshall Plan emerged. The Soviets pressured eastern European countries to create communist governments, and in the case of Czechoslovakia the communist party created enough disorder to scare its president into allowing a communist government to be formed. The USA responded by discussing with Britain the idea of a military alliance in western Europe and this eventually led to the North

? WHAT IF...

the superpowers had been less suspicious?

If the two superpowers had been less suspicious of each other perhaps the Cold War could have been prevented. Stalin could have accepted the Marshall Plan instead of viewing it as an American ploy to dominate Europe and threaten the USSR. The Truman administration could have tried to understand the Soviet Union's need to defend itself against another invasion, instead of acting as if the USSR was intent on taking over the world and threatening America. Perhaps the leaders of the two superpowers were too alike and too willing to see the world from only their points of view. Were the superpowers too quick to act in ways that were seen by the other side as threatening, and too stubborn to make concessions and reach an agreement? Or were they acting in the best interests of their country?

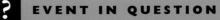

Atlantic Treaty Organization (NATO) in 1949. Six years later the Soviet Union formed the Warsaw Pact, a similar military grouping based around the USSR and the eastern European states with communist governments.

THE DIVISION OF GERMANY INTO EAST AND WEST

Events in Germany made it clear that Europe was being divided into a pro-American part and a pro-USSR part. The hostility that was developing between the USA and the USSR led to Germany being divided into two different states, East Germany and West Germany. By 1949, the USSR had its own nuclear weapons. By this time, the stage was set for an international conflict and the Cold War was underway.

? EVENT IN QUESTION

Dividing Germany: who was responsible?

In 1948, a new common currency was introduced in the western half of Germany, with the support of the USA. The Soviets replied by introducing a currency of their own. The USSR, applying pressure in order to prevent the western currency being used in Berlin, stopped food and supplies from western Germany reaching the west of Berlin. The USA responded by flying in the necessary supplies until the blockade was lifted. From one point of view, the USSR showed its aggressive intentions by blockading the west of Berlin. From another point of view, the USSR was provoked by the threat of a new currency that would bring all of Berlin under Western, non-Soviet, influence. Either way, Germany was divided into a Communist East Germany and a capitalist West Germany.

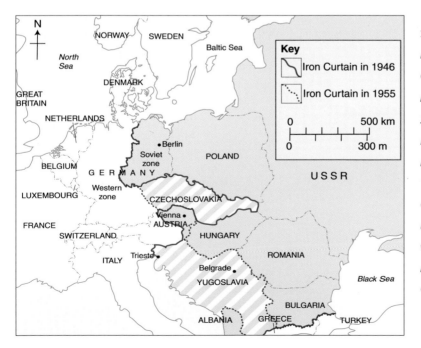

LEFT *The British Prime Minister, Winston Churchill, described the border between the Soviet-dominated Eastern Europe and the rest of Europe as an 'Iron Curtain'. By 1955, Czechoslovakia was under Soviet control while Yugoslavia has become an independent Communist state.*

CHAPTER 2

Theatres of War

The scene of action in a war is sometimes described as a theatre of war and, because the Cold War was played out in a variety of places and situations, many different theatres of war developed. Often only one of the two superpowers was involved in a theatre of war, using force to protect what it regarded as its area of influence. This was the case in Eastern Europe and in parts of South and Central America and Africa. In some places – Cuba being the most dramatic example – both the US and the USSR found themselves directly involved. In this kind of situation there was always the possibility that the theatre of war would broaden into a direct and very dangerous conflict between the two superpowers.

BELOW *Soviet troops and tanks entered Budapest, the capital of Hungary, in November 1956. In the street fighting that followed around 3,500 Hungarians were killed and 200,000 fled the country.*

Both Cold War superpowers used their military power to control neighbouring states. In 1956, when Hungary tried to establish an independent non-Communist government, Nikita Kruschev, leader of the Soviet Union, sent in tanks and thousands of Hungarians were killed. When in 1968 some Communist leaders, in what was then Czechoslovakia, tried to introduce liberal reforms, Soviet tanks once more rolled into the country and took control. The USA did not intervene in either of these situations, accepting the fact that these countries came under the Soviet sphere of control. In a similar way, the USSR did not intervene when the USA, feeling that Central America was its own sphere of influence, acted there to protect its interests. In 1965 the Dominican Republic was successfully invaded to restore a government friendly towards America. In 1983 the Caribbean island of Grenada was also invaded because its new government was regarded as unfriendly to the USA.

BELOW *A force of nearly 2,000 US troops invaded Grenada in 1983, resulting in some 400 Grenadian casualties and a new pro-American government.*

? EVENT IN QUESTION

The Berlin Wall: a safeguard against war?

Although the Wall changed the lives of many East Germans, Berliners had little choice but to accept its existence. Much of the rest of the world regarded the Wall as a physical symbol of the tyrannical nature of Communism. However, it was also seen as a way of avoiding a direct military confrontation between the two superpowers. While the Wall separated families and friends and limited personal freedoms, it also kept the armed forces of the USA and the USSR apart. Some people felt that the chances of an open war were therefore reduced.

THE BERLIN WALL

While the Marshall Plan helped West Germany's economy to prosper, East Germany suffered from a lack of investment and the economy never flourished. This made many East Germans want to leave for West Germany. It was not an easy task because barbed wire fences with armed guards, erected by East Germany, marked the boundary between the two parts of Germany. Within Berlin, however, people could move between the different sectors with little difficulty. The easiest way for East Germans to leave their country was by slipping into East Berlin and then crossing over to the western part of the city.

As refugees, the East Germans could either stay in West Berlin or ask to be flown out to other West German cities. By 1961, nearly three million citizens had left East Germany and, if this was allowed to continue, there was a danger of the East German economy collapsing altogether. The Soviet leader, Nikita Krushchev, met the new American President, John F. Kennedy, in June 1961 but they were unable to reach any agreement over Berlin. Within a couple of months, the

RIGHT *Conrad Schumann, a 19-year-old soldier reporting for duty as an East German border guard on 15 August 1961, took his chance to escape to the West when the other guards had their backs turned. He joined his family, who had fled earlier.*

East German government began building a barrier of barbed wire between the two halves of Berlin. This soon became a wall, with armed guards under orders to shoot anyone who tried to leave East Berlin without permission. Berlin was to remain a divided city for the next 28 years.

? PEOPLE IN QUESTION

Nikita Khruschev (1894–1971)

There are differences of opinion about the role of Nikita Khruschev, a leader of the USSR (1953-64), in the Cold War. While he made some steps towards giving his people more freedom, such as releasing political prisoners, he was also determined to maintain control over Eastern Europe. Like US President John Kennedy, Khruschev had some advisers who wanted the USSR to adopt an aggressive attitude towards the US and meet any threats of force with a show of equal force. And like Kennedy, Khruschev sought out a peaceful compromise to the crisis that developed over Cuba (see pages 18-19). Khruschev's resolve to avoid war was seen, however, as a mark of weakness. Two years later, he fell from power after losing the support of political and military leaders in his own country.

A DIVIDED EUROPE

In time, the division of Europe as a whole came to be regarded as an unavoidable consequence of the Cold War. The international borders that divided Western Europe from Eastern Europe were accepted as representing the division of the continent into areas of American and Soviet influence. Each side protected its territory with powerful armies numbered in millions and each side was in possession of fearsome nuclear weapons. A very dangerous kind of stability emerged, mainly because it came to be accepted that any military showdown in Europe would very probably see the destruction of the continent in a nuclear war. This never came to happen but many other parts of the world did become theatres of war, and in the case of Cuba it came close to a direct, armed conflict between the superpowers.

THE CUBAN MISSILE CRISIS

The USSR claimed that land on their side of the Iron Curtain should remain under Soviet influence. In a similar kind of way, the USA regarded the islands in the Caribbean Sea as land that should remain under their influence. This attitude on the part of the USA went back to long before the Cold War. So when in 1959 a corrupt dictatorship ruling Cuba was overthrown in a popular revolution, the USA was concerned over the island's future. This was especially true when Cuba's new socialist government, under its leader Fidel Castro, nationalized parts of the economy in which American companies had invested.

In March 1961, the CIA organized an invasion of Cuba by 1,500 Cuban exiles to depose Castro, but it was a complete failure. The USA cut off trade with Cuba, and so Castro looked to the USSR as a trading partner. What happened next was a major incident in the Cold War, and one that very nearly brought about World War III.

The USA had nuclear weapons in Italy and Britain and some fairly obsolete ones in Turkey, a country that shared a border with the USSR. In 1961, Castro agreed to Khruschev's plan to secretly place Soviet nuclear missiles in Cuba. US leaders grew alarmed when they discovered that Soviet ships were bringing missiles to Cuba. Any missiles launched from Cuba would

BELOW *Fidel Castro (seated), photographed in 1957 in the Sierra Maestra mountains in Cuba, a campaign that ended with the removal of Fulgencio Batista, a corrupt dictator who had ruled the island for twenty-five years.*

be close enough to the Unites States to have a direct hit. America responded by declaring a state of nuclear readiness, preparing its armoury for nuclear war and mounting a blockade of the sea so that no more Soviet ships carrying missiles could reach Cuba. The ships had orders to continue on their course, and a confrontation leading to war seemed about to happen.

The world held its breath as the superpower leaders discussed what to do. After many days of uncertainty, a deal was struck. The missiles were withdrawn by the Soviet Union in return for a guarantee by the US not to invade Cuba. Also, although this was kept secret from the public, the US agreed to later withdraw its own missiles from Turkey. Both the American and Soviet public saw the removal of the missiles from Cuba as a humiliating defeat for the USSR.

BELOW *Kennedy and Khruschev shake hands at a summit meeting in Vienna in June 1961. Within 18 months they were on the verge of unleashing World War III.*

? WHAT IF...

Kennedy and Khruschev had not made a deal?

At some stage, nuclear weapons would probably have been used. Which side might have first fired a nuclear weapon seems irrelevant given the mutual destruction it would have unleashed. The avoidance of war was a very close call. The US Defense Secretary McNamara later recalled leaving a crisis meeting 'on a beautiful fall evening ... into the open air to look and to smell it, because I thought it was the last Saturday I would ever see.' That same evening, one of Khruschev's advisers, convinced that Moscow would be hit by nuclear bombs, telephoned his wife to warn her to leave the city immediately.

CENTRAL AND SOUTH AMERICA

The Cuban crisis was unusual because it led to a direct confrontation between the USA and the USSR, and raised the stakes of the Cold War by making a nuclear war the likely outcome of such a confrontation. For the most part, however, the Cold War was played out across the world in a less spectacular manner. Central and South America became one such theatre of war, lasting from the 1950s right through to the 1990s.

GUATEMALA

Central and South America became involved in the Cold War in 1954 when the CIA successfully deposed the elected government of Guatemala. Large areas of uncultivated land belonging mostly to an American company had been nationalized in Guatemala and distributed to landless peasants. The CIA trained and financed a force of Guatemalans who overthrew the government and installed a military dictator in power. The nationalized land was taken back and hundreds of left-wing supporters were executed.

RIGHT *Many of the independent states of Central America, partly because of their proximity to the USA, became battlegrounds during the course of the Cold War.*

CHILE

Something similar took place in Chile, where a socialist government under President Salvador Allende was elected in 1970. Land was nationalized and distributed to poor farmers, and industries were also nationalized. The USA worked secretly to destabilize the country, prevent economic assistance reaching the government and encourage a military overthrow of Allende. In 1973 there was a military takeover by General Pinochet, Allende was killed and hundreds of thousands of left-wing supporters were rounded up. There were many executions of supporters and many more were never seen again, becoming known as 'the disappeared'. As in Guatemala, the nationalized land was taken away from farmers under Pinochet's military rule and nationalized industries were returned to their private owners.

Augusto Pinochet (1915 –)

After overthrowing President Allende, Augusto Pinochet closed the Chilean parliament and established a military regime. More than 3,000 Allende supporters are believed to have been killed by Pinochet's forces, and thousands more tortured. However, Pinochet always maintained that he acted as a patriot and rescued his country from the threat of communism. As Chile's economy improved, many Chileans came to support this view. In October 1998 Pinochet was arrested on charges relating to human rights abuses during his years of power. The case was suspended in July 2001 due to his ill-health.

BELOW: *General Pinochet, who ruled Chile between 1973 and 1990 after deposing the elected government, boasted in 1975, 'Never a leaf moves in Chile without my knowing of it.'*

NICARAGUA

BELOW *The group that opposed Nicaragua's left-wing government were* contrarevolutionarios *and they became known as the Contras. With US aid, they grew from a force of a few hundred to about 15,000 between 1982 and 1985.*

In Nicaragua, the largest country in Central America, the US had an ally in the Somoza government. The Somoza family ruled over an extremely poor country and became very rich through corruption. By 1979, after a bitter civil war, Somoza was overthrown and a left-wing government was formed by the rebels, the Sandinistas. They set about improving life for Nicaraguans and received support from Cuba. By 1981, another civil war had broken out and the Contras, a group trying to depose the Sandinistas, turned to the US for support. The CIA armed and trained the Contras and in 1984

organized a plot to mine the ports of Nicaragua. This resulted in damage to ships of other countries and the American Congress publicly withdrew support from the Contras. By secretly selling arms to Iran and using the money to aid the Contras, however, the White House maintained its policy of opposing the Sandinistas. This illegal operation, when it became known to the public in 1986, became known as the Iran-Contra scandal and caused severe embarrassment to the US government.

EL SALVADOR

El Salvador, also in Central America, had a similar history to Nicaragua. A harsh military government was supported by the USA while a rebel army waged a guerrilla war. Many thousands of people were killed, or became part of 'the disappeared' as a result of government 'death squads', and a civil war lasted for years with neither side able to achieve a decisive victory. In 1981, the military government received $36 million of aid from the US and three years later this had risen to $197 million.

The civil war lasted 12 years and did not come to an end until 1992, after an estimated 75,000 people had been killed and $6 billion had been spent by the US in aiding the rebels. El Salvador is now a democratic republic and the rebel army of the civil war period is a political party.

US intervention in Central and South America; was the Cold War an excuse?

From one point of view, the Cold War was used by the USA as an excuse in Central and South America to depose any government that was not friendly to American business interests. Many countries in that part of the world suffered from poverty and from enormous differences between rich and poor, and American-owned companies were seen to benefit from such inequalities. When left-wing governments tried to improve the lives of their citizens, the USA used the Cold War as an excuse to remove them from power, even if they were democratically elected. From another point of view, however, the USA was protecting its interests in an unstable part of the world where communism was a threat. Left-wing governments, it was argued, would not support the USA and would instead turn to the USSR for support. This, it was felt, would tip the world balance of power in favour of the USSR and ought to be resisted. Therefore, it was necessary to support governments friendly to the US, even if they were brutal dictatorships.

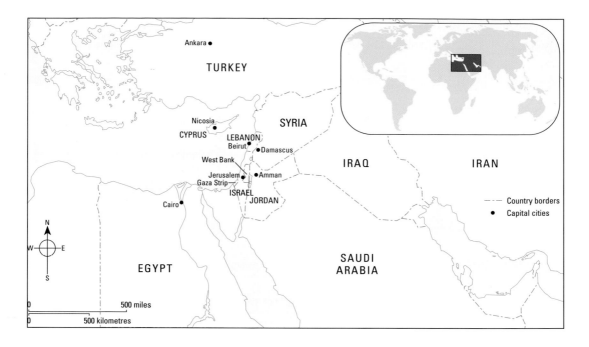

Ankara ●

TURKEY

Nicosia
CYPRUS

SYRIA

LEBANON
Beirut ●
● Damascus

West Bank

IRAQ

IRAN

Jerusalem
Gaza Strip
ISRAEL
● Amman
Cairo ●
JORDAN

--- Country borders
● Capital cities

N
W ⊕ E
S

EGYPT

SAUDI
ARABIA

500 miles

500 kilometres

ABOVE *Most of the Middle East was affected by the course of the Cold War. The West Bank and the Gaza Strip are Palestinian territories but under the military control of Israel.*

THE MIDDLE EAST

The Cold War in Central and South America was affected by the region's closeness to the North American mainland, and by US economic interests in that part of the world. In another theatre of war, the Middle East, both the USA and the USSR shared similar concerns because of the region's rich supply of oil. In Iran in 1953, the CIA helped a USA-friendly party to depose the government and take power. The USA provided military and economic assistance and, in return, American oil companies and military advisers had a large presence in the country. This arrangement lasted until 1979 when a non-Communist but anti-American Islamic government, under Ayatollah Khomeini, took power in Iran.

ISRAEL

The USA also sought to make an ally of the state of Israel, a country that had come into existence in 1948. This angered Arab states, especially the Palestinians whose land had been used to create the state of Israel. The stateless Palestinians lost more land in an Arab-Israeli war in 1967 and began to blame the USA, who went on to support Israel with massive military and

? **EVENT IN QUESTION**

War in the Middle East: a consequence of the Cold War?

From one point of view, the Middle East was an unstable part of the world where the USSR sought to exercise its influence and have a say over a region that provided a major source of oil throughout the world. The USA supported Israel and built up its military strength so that the country could function as a deterrent to any Soviet plans for expansion in the Middle East. Therefore, war in the Middle East was a consequence of the Cold War. From another point of view, the Cold War was only part of the background and the underlying conflict arose from the determination of both the USA and the USSR to try and maintain control over a valuable source of oil. Support for this point of view comes from the fact that the end of the Cold War did not bring war in the Middle East to an end. It is also true, however, that the situation in the Middle East is very complex and goes beyond the more straightforward conflict that fuelled the Cold War.

economic aid. The USSR, meanwhile, sought to make allies of states such as Syria and Egypt through offers of aid and, in this way, the Middle East became another stage for the conduct of the Cold War. Another war between Israel, Syria and Egypt in 1973 saw the opposing sides being armed and supported by the rival superpowers.

LEFT *Two US-made Israeli tanks patrol East Jerusalem on 10 June 1967, six days after Israel launched an attack that led to the occupation of the Gaza Strip, the Golan Heights of Syria, and the West Bank and Arab sector of East Jerusalem.*

WAR IN AFRICA

Africa also became a focus for the deadly drama of the Cold War and, as with the Middle East, it had the effect of turning parts of the region into another theatre of war. During the 1950s and 1960s over thirty new countries emerged in Africa as former colonial powers such as Britain bowed out in the face of demands for independence. The superpowers, each fearing that the other side would gain influence and power in the region, stepped in and chose different sides as allies. In the case of Angola in 1975, communist China as well as the USA and the USSR became involved in a conflict that cost

LEFT *Early days in Angola's civil war, which lasted from 1975 to 2002.*

many thousands of lives. The three powers gave military aid to different sides in a civil war that broke out in the country. Cuba and South Africa also became involved by sending in troops that fought with one another.

THE ANC AND SOUTH AFRICA

The USSR was able to appeal to nationalist groups in different parts of Africa on the grounds that communism supported their claims for independence and equality. This resulted in the African National Congress (ANC), a guerrilla force opposed to the white minority ruling South Africa, regarding the USSR as more of an ally than the US. Another result was that the USA remained on close terms with a racist state that denied equal rights to the black majority population (see panel) in a system called apartheid.

? WHAT IF...

The Cold War had never reached South Africa?

It is possible that, without the Cold War, apartheid would have ended in South Africa sooner than it finally did in the early 1990s. While the Cold War lasted, the USA felt there was a good reason to support South Africa, because it defended capitalism and allied itself with the West. Towards the end of the 1980s, when the Cold War was drawing to a close, the attitude of the USA, as well as other Western countries and international banks, started to change. They began to apply pressure on the white South African government to dismantle the system of apartheid and reach an agreement with the ANC.

The drawing to a close of the Cold War also changed the ANC. Some groups within the African National Congress loosened their attachment to the USSR and the economic policies of the ANC became less socialist. This did a great deal to convince the white government in South Africa that a peace agreement could be reached with the ANC.

CHAPTER 3

The Cold War in Asia

The Cold War had its origins in the state of Europe after World War II but, as has been seen, the conflict between the superpowers was also acted out in other parts of the world. Apart from nearly 200 people who were killed trying to cross the Berlin Wall, very few people died as a result of the Cold War in Europe. On the other hand, in addition to the hundreds of thousands killed in Central and South America and Africa, the number of victims who died on Cold War battlefields in Asia is counted in millions. It was in Asia that the Cold War created the conditions for open and prolonged warfare, bringing death and destruction on a massive scale.

BELOW *During the Cold War, Russia, Kazakhstan, Uzbekistan, Kyrgyzstan, Turkmenistan and Tajikistan were all part of the USSR.*

ABOVE *US troops waiting for action atop an M26 tank in Korea in 1950.*

CHANGES IN ASIA

An important reason why the Cold War made itself felt so intensely in Asia is the history of that part of the world. Before World War II much of the region had been colonized by European powers, but by 1945 the situation had changed radically. By successfully invading South-east Asia, the Japanese had exposed the weaknesses of European military control over its colonies. So although Japan was eventually defeated, many Asian nations sought independence after World War II.

Former colonial rulers, mainly Britain and France, were no longer able to govern their empires as they once had. The region became unstable because the nature of the new governments that would replace the colonial powers remained uncertain.

? EVENT IN QUESTION

The end of colonialism in Asia

In its own way, the course of the Second World War set the stage for the Cold War in Asia just as it had done in Europe. Although finally defeated in 1945, Japan had launched a devastating attack on British Malaya in 1941 and captured the British-controlled island of Singapore early the following year. British prestige was dealt a severe blow because the Japanese had shown that Asians could defeat a Western imperial power. When the war was over, countries such as Vietnam and India, realizing that they need not remain the colonies of Western countries, began to demand independence. The cost of the war had weakened Britain and France financially and they found it difficult, after 1945, to bear the additional costs of resisting independence movements. This was the background to the instability in Asia and it provided more theatres of war for the Cold War.

COMMUNISM IN ASIA

BELOW *Celebrations in Tiananmen Square in Beijing on 1 October 1952, marking the third anniversary of Mao Zedong's announcement in the same square that 'the Chinese people have now stood up'.*

The largest of the unstable states in south-east Asia was China, a country that Japan had invaded and tried to control in the 1930s. In 1949 China became an independent Communist state and its leader, Mao Zedong, quickly established warm relations with the USSR. The prospect of an alliance between these two powerful states alarmed the West considerably, though, as it turned out, the USSR and China would later fall out with one another. Equally alarming for the West was the fact that leaders of other national independence movements in Asia, seeking to replace the injustice of colonial rule, found a model for their hopes in the ideas of Communism. In this way, their nationalist struggles for independence became entangled in the Cold War conflict.

WAR IN KOREA

The first Asian country to suffer as a result of the Cold War was Korea. The country had been a Japanese colony during World War II, before being liberated by Soviet and US forces in 1945. They divided the country and a Communist government ruled the north while a non-Communist government was established in the south. North Korea became an ally of the USSR and its leader, Kim Il Sung, sought permission from Stalin to invade the south and unify the country as a Communist state. This took place on 25 June 1950 and the USA reacted by calling on the United Nations (UN) to condemn the invasion.

At the time the USSR was boycotting the UN because Communist China was not being admitted as a member, and on 27 June the UN voted to defend South Korea by military force. The US, along with Britain and other allies, sent troops to fight the North Korean army and a period of bitter warfare followed. By October, the scale of the war increased dramatically when China sent its own forces into the conflict. General MacArthur, commanding US troops in Korea, was dismissed from his post after calling for the invasion and bombing of China.

? PEOPLE IN QUESTION

Douglas MacArthur
(1880–1964)

General Douglas MacArthur, a celebrated hero of World War II, was placed in charge of military forces in Korea. He had always argued that the Cold War would be fought in Asia rather than Europe and he welcomed the opportunity to prosecute a determined war against the enemy. Applying the logic of the Cold War, he called for the bombing of China as a way of achieving success in Korea. However, political leaders on both sides of the Cold War were learning to avoid an open war that might be difficult for either side to win. A general like MacArthur, who saw the Cold War in very military terms, was not acceptable and he was dismissed. To some, MacArthur was a Cold War hero who spoke his mind; to others, MacArthur was a dangerous Cold War warrior who risked nuclear war.

EVENT IN QUESTION

Did the Korean War achieve anything?

From one perspective, the invasion of South Korea was viewed as a clear instance of Soviet expansion that needed to be contained. If the invasion was not resisted militarily, it was reasoned, the Soviet Union would feel free to organize similar take-overs in other parts of Asia. From another perspective, however, it was only North Korea that wanted to invade in order to unify the country, and the USSR agreed to their ally's wish because they didn't think the USA would go to war over it. The USSR had no plan to expand its influence and dominate the region. Neither the USSR or China wanted a war over Korea and both were happy to reach an agreement that ended the conflict.

COUNTING THE COST

The Cold War was played out in a deadly land and air war in Korea. Soviet MiG-15 fighter planes, some piloted by Soviet pilots, fought American F-86 Sabers. Terrible atrocities occurred on both sides, and the US Air Force dropped almost as many bombs on the cities of North Korea as had been dropped on Germany over the entire course of World War II. Peace talks began in late 1951 and dragged on until a final ceasefire took effect in July of 1953. Millions of Korean civilians and

BELOW *UN soldiers head north to engage in fighting while Korean civilians flee south with their possessions to escape the battlefront.*

soldiers, at least a quarter of a million Chinese, over 54,000 Americans, and 3,000 other UN troops, all lost their lives in the war.

War in Vietnam

Beginning shortly after the Korean War, the USA became involved in another part of Asia for much the same reason that had led to their presence in Korea. The country this time was Vietnam, a former French colony that was divided into two halves in 1954 after France suffered a military defeat by Vietnamese rebels fighting for independence. The northern half of the country came under a Communist government, while the southern half of the country was left in the hands of non-Communist Vietnamese groups who had backed France. South Vietnam, an undemocratic state where elections never took place, was sponsored by the US, who wanted to contain the spread of communism in South-east Asia.

A guerrilla war developed as Vietnamese rebels sought to unite the south of the country with the north. In 1965, the US sent marines to the south of Vietnam and by the end of the year, with over 200,000 American troops in the country, the Vietnam War had begun. Nationalist forces supporting North Vietnam, in both halves of the country, became known as the Viet Cong.

RA SỨC RÈN LUYỆN QUÂN SỰ
SẴN SÀNG BẢO VỆ TỔ QUỐC

RIGHT *This poster, published in North Vietnam in the middle of the Vietnam War, appealed to nationalist feelings with the words, 'Strive to train soldiers to defend the nation.'*

33

The Domino Theory: a myth?

The fall of one domino can have a knock-on effect on a whole row of dominoes. This example was used to argue that the loss of one state to Soviet Communism would lead to eventual domination by the USSR of a whole series of countries. Such a domino theory became the logic for conducting the war in Vietnam and for the Cold War as a whole, but the logic has been questioned by many historians. The Viet Cong were not Soviet puppets but nationalists who fought to remove foreign powers from their land. It is also pointed out that although the Viet Cong were victorious this did not have the destabilizing effect in South-east Asia that many predicted. One domino fell but it did not lead to a collapse of the whole row of dominoes. Some people claim the domino theory was an excuse for the USA to try and dominate the world.

THE CONFLICT CONTINUES

American involvement in Vietnam gradually increased in its scope and by 1967 there were over 400,000 American troops in South Vietnam. Meanwhile, the Viet Cong received assistance from China and the Soviet Union.

The launch of a major offensive by the Viet Cong in 1968, the Tet offensive, proved to be a failure but its large scale and the unexpected nature of the attack convinced many US leaders that the war was unwinnable. It took another five years before this was generally accepted in the US and a peace settlement was finally agreed in 1973. Two years later South Vietnam was invaded and overrun by the North Vietnamese and the country was unified as a single Communist country.

A COSTLY FAILURE

American involvement in Vietnam was largely viewed as a failure, both internationally and within the USA. It raised moral questions about American policy towards small, developing countries that bore the brunt of Cold War hostilities. Moral questions were also raised when it became known that US leaders had agreed to heavy bombing of Cambodia and Laos, (neighbours of Vietnam that the North Vietnamese used for their supply lines) without the knowledge of the American public. The deaths of thousands of American soldiers came to be seen by many as pointless and unnecessary. In the USA itself, young people rebelled when conscripted to fight in a war in which they did not believe.

Ho Chi Minh
(1892-1969)

Ho Chi Minh was the leader of the Viet Cong who fought the Americans in Vietnam. During the 1960s he was viewed by many in the West as a dangerous enemy, dedicated to spreading communism across Southeast Asia. Today, many historians regard Ho Chi Minh as first and foremost a nationalist who wanted Vietnam to be an independent country. He was a Communist but not one who worked for the USSR in the Cold War. He did seek support from both the USSR and China but only because he needed their support in his country's struggle for independence.

ABOVE *A Vietnamese mother and her children swim across a river at Quinhon in South Vietnam to escape an American air strike at the start of the Vietnam War in 1965.*

WAR IN AFGHANISTAN

The events in Afghanistan are an example of how the post-Vietnam Cold War was conducted by the USA and the USSR. In 1979 Afghanistan was ruled by a Communist government that did not have the support of Afghans and was propped up by the USSR. The USA gave secret support to Afghan opposition and, in order to crush this opposition, the USSR sent in troops to occupy the country.

A bitter civil war developed, with the CIA providing many millions of dollars to the Mujahedeen, the name of the Islamic fighters who resisted the Soviet occupation. The national security adviser to the US President at that

BELOW *Soviet troops in Afghanistan, two days after the first and only violation of a neutral border by the USSR during the Cold War.*

time, Jimmy Carter, later spoke of giving the USSR its own Vietnam, and the Soviet experience in Afghanistan did have similarities with American involvement in Vietnam. In both conflicts, the invading forces gradually became more and more committed to a guerrilla war that they couldn't win.

By the end of 1982, nearly 5,000 Soviet soldiers had died in Afghanistan and the USSR was ready to withdraw. The war did not end, however, until the Cold War itself drew to a close. The Mujahedeen carried on fighting, this time amongst themselves, until a group known as the Taliban emerged to rule most of the country and form their own government.

ABOVE *The Mujahedeen, 'soldiers of God' rebelled against a left-wing government in Afghanistan that encouraged women to join literacy classes. They recruited boys and armed them with AK-47 rifles.*

? EVENT IN QUESTION

The rise of the Taliban: a result of the Cold War?

From one point of view, the Taliban was a group of ruthless and extremist Afghan fighters. As rulers of Afghanistan, they were heavily financed by Osama bin Laden, a wealthy Saudi Arabian who became fiercely anti-American. Some historians argue that the Taliban was a monster hatched by the Cold War. If the USSR and the USA had not turned Afghanistan into a theatre of war, it is unlikely that an extremist group like the Taliban would ever have emerged. Those Mujahedeen who became the Taliban were united by Islam and a common desire to expel Soviet troops. One reason they grew strong was because of the funding they received from the USA in the course of the Cold War.

CHAPTER 4

Living Through the Cold War

The Cuban missile crisis (see pages 18-19) had a sobering effect on both superpowers. If nuclear weapons were used by either side, the only certain result would be the death of millions. This led to a theory that nuclear peace could be maintained because of, and not merely in spite of, the certainty of mutually assured destruction (MAD). For many people living through the Cold War, the MAD theory came to seem an appropriate name for an insane state of affairs where the destruction of the planet was the only certain outcome of World War III.

A BREAK IN HOSTILITIES

Some periods of the Cold War promised the possibility of peaceful co-existence between the superpowers. One such period came after the superpowers accepted a divided Europe, a divided Germany and a divided city of Berlin. In 1958, at the start of what would be a three-year period free of nuclear testing, negotiations for a test ban treaty got underway but failed because the two sides could not agree over how best to proceed. Meetings between the USSR and the USA took place in the early 1970s and led to the signing of two treaties in 1972. They were known as SALT-1, (Strategic Arms Limitation Talks) and limited the quantity of nuclear weapons each side could stockpile. Further agreements led to a SALT-II treaty in 1979, but by this time

? WHAT IF...

there was a Dr Strangelove?

In 1964, a Hollywood film was released called *Dr Strangelove, or How I Learned to Stop Worrying and Love the Bomb*. The film imagined the commander of a US air base going insane and ordering a nuclear attack on the USSR. The attack is cancelled but, due to a series of mishaps, one bomber plane cannot be recalled. The Soviets are warned but they are unable to prevent their own defence system, a 'Doomsday machine', from automatically releasing nuclear weapons as a response to being attacked. The film ends with a series of nuclear explosions and the audience imagines the end of the world. Critics of the film insisted that, in the real world, safety features would ensure that such a catastrophic situation could never take place. Others argued that a Doomsday machine was technically possible and that the likelihood of a terrible mistake being made was always a real possibility.

the Cold War was heating up again and the treaty was never ratified by the US Senate.

In the USA, a more aggressive attitude towards the USSR became associated with Reagan's election as president in 1980. The USSR was also shifting to a more hostile attitude towards the USA. Both sides began developing new nuclear weapons systems: the SS-20 missiles by the Soviets, and Pershing-2 and Cruise missiles by the Americans. In the early 1980s, the Reagan administration engaged the USSR in an intensive arms race and announced plans to develop a new defence system against incoming missiles, popularly known as 'Star Wars'.

ABOVE *US President Richard Nixon and Russian Communist Party leader Leonid Brezhnev shake hands after signing the SALT-1 treaty in 1972.*

39

PROPAGANDA WAR

Throughout the Cold War a propaganda war developed between the two superpowers. This involved each side seeking to portray itself as morally superior to the other. The USA represented itself as standing for freedom in the face of a Soviet Communist dictatorship that denied human rights. The USSR represented itself as standing for a just society in the face of a capitalist America that placed profit above equality.

Words and images, including books and films, became the weapons of the propaganda war. In the USSR, books and films were promoted that focused on social injustices in the West such as racial inequality and poverty. Books by a Russian author, Aleksandr Solzhenitsyn, that featured Soviet prison camps and the abuse of state power, were translated into English and widely promoted in the West. Some of the most widely read novels in the West were Cold War thrillers, featuring spies and traitors, which usually portrayed the 'baddies' as working for the USSR and the 'goodies' as working for the West.

BELOW *This 1957 advertisement for American Convair F-102A jet planes, like the Soviet cartoon on page five, is an example of the propaganda war that was an essential part of the Cold War.*

Freedom Has a New Sound!

ALL OVER AMERICA these days the blast of supersonic flight is shattering the old familiar sounds of city and countryside.
At U.S. Air Force bases strategically located near key cities our Airmen maintain their *round the clock* vigil, ready to take off on a moment's notice in jet aircraft like Convair's F-102A all-weather interceptor. Every flight has only one purpose—your personal protection!
The next time jets thunder overhead, remember that the pilots who fly them are not willful disturbers of your peace; they are patriotic young Americans affirming *your New Sound of Freedom!*

PUBLISHED FOR BETTER UNDERSTANDING OF THE MISSION OF THE U.S.A.F. AIR DEFENSE COMMAND

CONVAIR

THE ENEMY WITHIN

In real life, some traitors were paid for betraying their government's secrets while others sincerely believed that they were working for a country that represented a better way of life. Early on in the Cold War, there were Soviet spies with high-ranking positions in the British secret service. Men such as Guy Burgess and Kim Philby passed on valuable secrets to the KGB, the Soviet equivalent of the CIA. Later in the Cold War, Oleg Gordievsky, working for the KGB in London, passed valuable information to the West. People lost their lives as a result of spying. Philby passed on details of agents working for the West, who were caught and shot. In

America, Ethel and Julius Rosenberg were executed in the electric chair after being found guilty of passing atomic secrets to the USSR.

? EVENT IN QUESTION

Flight 007: who was at fault?

In August 1983 a Korean Airlines passenger plane, Flight 007, was shot down with the loss of 269 lives. A Soviet fighter plane brought down the jumbo jet, which was 587 kilometres off course and inside a sensitive area of Soviet air space. The incident was highly controversial because, while the US condemned it as a terrorist attack, the USSR accused the US of using the passenger plane as part of a spying mission. There was a US surveillance plane in the area at the time and tapes later revealed that the jumbo jet repeatedly ignored warnings from the Soviet fighter plane, even after shots were fired across it. What was the real cause of the shooting down of Flight 007? The truth may never emerge.

BELOW *The family of a Flight 007 victim, shown in her college graduation photograph, grieves at a altar memorial at Seoul airport in South Korea.*

THE HOUSE UN-AMERICAN ACTIVITIES COMMITTEE

During the Cold War, some American citizens found themselves accused of being sympathetic to the USSR. In the 1950s in the USA, the House Un-American Activities Committee (HUAC) publicly investigated people working in Hollywood who might be sympathetic to communism. The Federal Bureau of Investigation (FBI), headed by J. Edgar Hoover, also dedicated itself to exposing such people, though in a less public manner. Citizens suspected by HUAC or the FBI of being sympathetic to communism, 'reds under the bed' as they were called, were likely to lose their jobs and find themselves prevented from finding similar work elsewhere.

Citizens in the USSR and Eastern Europe who were under suspicion of not being loyal enough to the Soviet government were also investigated by government departments. The penalties were far more severe than in the USA. Hundreds of thousands of people were sent to labour camps and, before Stalin died in 1953, many citizens whose loyalty was questioned were executed by the state.

CITIZENS PROTEST

In Western Europe, an area very likely to be targeted in the event of total war, people began to protest against nuclear weapons. In 1958 in London, the Campaign for Nuclear Disarmament (CND) was founded and it called for the removal of nuclear weapons from Britain. Similar campaigns were organized in other parts of Europe and by the late 1970s, when American missiles were being based in Western Europe, anti-nuclear movements were growing in strength. In the USA the focus of citizen protest was against the Vietnam War, a war that many Americans came to regard as not only unwinnable but also as unjustifiable. In October 1967 some 75,000 protestors marched against it in Washington.

? EVENT IN QUESTION

Anti-nuclear demonstrators: Soviet puppets?

The anti-nuclear movements that developed across Western Europe in the late 1970s and early 1980s did not choose sides in the Cold War. They felt that the existence of large numbers of American Cruise missiles in Europe was a threat to the chance of peace. Critics of anti-nuclear movements claimed that such movements only served to weaken the West's ability to win the Cold War. It was said that the Soviet Union was happy to support such movements for just such a reason. Peace protestors argued that the removal of the missiles would encourage the Soviets to do the same. On the other side critics argued that pacifist protestors were being manipulated by Soviet intelligence.

BELOW *Thousands of people regularly gathered outside the US Air Force Base at Greenham Common in England, to protest at the installation of nuclear missiles. A women's peace camp was established there as a focus for anti-nuclear protests.*

CHAPTER 5

The End of the Cold War

I n the decade after 1975, when mistrust between the superpowers reached a high level, many people wondered how the Cold War could ever come to a peaceful end, let alone when that might happen. Although both superpowers were spending more money on weapons than ever before, the arms race was proving to be more of a burden to the Soviets than it was to the USA.

GORBACHEV BREAKS THE ICE

The American economy was much stronger than the Soviet one and the USA could better afford the high cost of increased military spending. The Soviets only weakened their economy further by trying to keep up with American levels of spending on military equipment. One solution was for the USSR to make drastic cuts in its military spending and channel what was saved into the domestic economy. This is what Mikhail Gorbachev, the new Soviet leader, decided had to be done.

? PEOPLE IN QUESTION

Mikhail Gorbachev
(1931–)

Unlike Stalin, Gorbachev was not a dictator and relied on popular support to push through the radical reforms being made to Soviet society. Like most national leaders, he also needed the support of other leaders and politicians. While he usually had both kinds of support, he also had to contend with conservative Communists who grew increasingly alarmed at the way the USSR seemed to be surrendering power to the traditional enemy. In August 1989, the Polish Communist leader telephoned Gorbachev to ask for advice about sharing government with non-Communists. A few days before the Berlin Wall came down, the East German leader also telephoned Gorbachev to ask for advice. On both occasions, Gorbachev's advice was to give way to popular demands. A different leader of the USSR might have advised the use of the military against the public.

The 1985 election of Mikhail Gorbachev as leader of the Communist Party in the USSR marks an important stage in the Cold War. Gorbachev represented a younger generation of Russians and was determined to confront the economic problems facing the USSR. He was a Communist who wanted to reform his country so that people could enjoy a higher standard of living. He introduced policies of *perestroika* (economic reform) and *glasnost* (openness) and began negotiations with the USA over the reduction of nuclear weapons. At the start of 1986, Gorbachev made proposals that astonished the rest of the world, speaking of the wish to eliminate all nuclear weapons. As a first step, he suggested the removal of all medium-range nuclear missiles from Europe, an idea that some in the West thought must be some kind of a trick.

BELOW *The traditional parade of Soviet armed power in Red Square took place as usual in 1985 but Gorbachev was ready to act on his declaration 'We want to stop and not continue the arms race.'*

ABOVE *After a morning meeting with President Reagan in Geneva in November 1985, Gorbachev called him a 'political dinosaur' but during the afternoon, in front of a log fire, they began to get along; it was the beginning of the end of the Cold War.*

LIFTING THE IRON CURTAIN

Before December 1987, when Gorbachev and Reagan met in Washington, the Soviet leader made it clear that he intended to withdraw from Afghanistan (see page 36). Partly as a result, a treaty was signed in Washington that removed all Soviet SS-20 missiles and all American Cruise and Pershing missiles from Europe.

At the end of 1988 Gorbachev astonished the world again by declaring to the UN that the Soviet army would be reduced by half a million men, and 50,000 soldiers would be removed from Eastern Europe. The consequences of this were profound because the Cold War had always been conducted by each side using military power, or the threat of such power, to maintain control over particular regions. Eastern Europe had been under Soviet control since the end of World War II but Gorbachev lifted the 'iron curtain' when he addressed the UN and said: 'Force or the threat of force neither can nor should be instruments of foreign policy ... Freedom of choice is a universal principle. It knows no exception.' Stressing that this applied 'both to the capitalist and socialist system', Gorbachev was virtually announcing the USSR's withdrawal from the Cold War.

? WHAT IF...

Gorbachev had not come to power?

What if there was no Gorbachev to meet President George Bush in 1989 and declare, 'We don't consider you as an enemy any more.'? In one sense it was clearly Gorbachev who bought the Cold War to an end because he took the initiative in ending the arms race and reducing the Soviet military presence in Eastern Europe. In another sense, it could be said that the Cold War was brought to an end by the failure of the Soviet economic system. Gorbachev, desperate to save his country's economy, was forced to end the Cold War because this was the only way to reduce the cost of the military budget. Would the Cold War have ended if Gorbachev had not been the leader of the USSR? What does seem likely is that, without Gorbachev, there would have been far less chance of the Cold War ending as peacefully as it did.

BELOW *Gorbachev and Reagan in Red Square, Moscow, 1988.*

Independence for Eastern Europe

The Cold War began to draw to a close in 1989 as countries in Eastern Europe realized the Soviet Union would not use force to maintain its control over them. By the summer of 1989, a non-Communist party was sharing power in Poland. By the middle of the year, three Baltic states inside the USSR - Lithuania, Latvia and Estonia - were demanding independence. The spirit of reform and change that Gorbachev had introduced was having unexpected consequences, as non-Russian states within the USSR called for independence.

The Wall Comes Down

The most dramatic consequence of Gorbachev's reforms was a series of events that led to the knocking down of the Berlin Wall, the most obvious symbol of the Cold War. It started with Hungary's decision to open its border with

BELOW *Drawing back the iron curtain, part one: in May 1989, Hungarian border guards cut and pull down the barbed wire fence dividing their country from Austria, allowing East Germans to travel through Czechoslovakia and into Austria via Hungary.*

LEFT *Drawing back the Iron Curtain, part two: in November 1989, the Berlin Wall is brought down for good. The Reichstag, the old German parliament, is in the background.*

non-Communist Austria, allowing East Germans to make their way to Hungary and then cross to the West. Some 13,000 people left within three days of the border opening in September 1989. What was happening in Hungary had a major effect on people in East Berlin who also wanted to travel to the West. Large crowds gathered in Berlin on the night of 9 November, after an announcement earlier in the day that visas would be granted to all citizens wishing to visit the West. On hearing this promise, people began to demand to cross immediately and some guards, not sure what to do, opened the gates in the Berlin Wall. Families that had been divided since the Wall went up in 1961 were reunited, and Berlin erupted into emotional celebrations as people began to physically dismantle the Wall.

? WHAT IF...

the Cold War never happened?

By the 1980s, some four decades into the Cold War, Soviet citizens often had to queue for essential food items and many consumer goods were in short supply. In the USA, where life expectancy for a black person in New York's Harlem was lower than some developing cities, the difference between the rich and poor was four times greater than in the USSR. If there had been no Cold War, would some of the trillions of dollars that went into military spending have been spent on problems like these? It is difficult to know, but what is sure is that many of the millions of people who died in conflicts fuelled by superpower rivalry would still be alive today if the Cold War had never taken place. Military spending became a national priority for the superpowers, at the expense of social and economic problems, and many other countries affected by the Cold War adopted a similar priority.

THE COLD WAR IS OVER

By the end of 1989, nearly every state in Eastern Europe allied to the USSR had removed its Communist rulers. It was remarkable that while many wars marked the course of the Cold War, its ending was brought about peacefully. Apart from violent events in Romania that led to the execution of the state's leader, Nicolae Ceausescu, the changes were largely achieved without bloodshed. After the fall of the Berlin Wall, dramatic events continued to unfold as the consequences of Gorbachev's reforms had more unexpected results.

By the middle of 1990, plans for the reunification of Germany had been drawn up and Gorbachev accepted that the country would become part of NATO. For many observers, this represented not just the end of the Cold War but the victory of the West. NATO had been formed as a military alliance against the USSR and now a united

BELOW *April 1991 and the journey home for Soviet missile launchers that had been based in Poland during the Cold War.*

Germany was going to join that alliance. At the height of the Cuban crisis, Khruschev had written an emotional letter to Kennedy in which he compared the Cold War to two men holding a rope with a knot tied in the middle: 'the more the two of us pull, the tighter the knot will be tied.' This is how the Cold War seemed to be until Gorbachev arrived on the scene and cut the knot.

BELOW *A portrait of Lenin, the first leader of the USSR, is deliberately spattered with red paint as a gesture of contempt by demonstrators outside the Communist Party building in Kiev, the capital of Ukraine, in August 1991. The Ukrainian demonstrators reaffirmed their country's declaration of independence from the USSR, first made in 1990.*

? EVENT IN QUESTION

The Cold War: who were the winners?

In many ways, the Cold War was won by the United States. Its economy was more able to support the increasing cost of an arms race and this was finally acknowledged by the USSR. The West also won the Cold War in the sense that the people of Eastern Europe chose not to support the Soviet Union and chose instead an economic and social system modelled on that of the USA. A different point of view points out that to speak of winning or losing is itself part of the confrontational vocabulary of the Cold War. Is talk of winning or losing a mature response when the Cold War threatened to destroy world civilization? Did the USSR achieve a moral victory by choosing to question what was more important – superpower status in a nuclear world or a more modest existence without the need for nuclear weapons?

CHAPTER 6

After the Cold War

BELOW *Russia, adopting the Western economic system after the break-up of the USSR, experienced food queues as wages failed to increase in line with price rises.*

It is not possible to pin down the start of the Cold War to one particular year. The end of World War II in 1945 marks its beginning, though some historians would go back to 1917 and the Russian Communist revolution. This revolution, it is said, marked the start of a deep conflict between two economic and social systems, a conflict that led to the Cold War when both the USA and the USSR became superpowers after 1945. The Cold War drew to a close between 1989 and 1991 as the events of those years dramatically changed the course of world history and ended more than 45 years of open conflict between the superpowers.

LEFT *Capitalism in Russia brought a new range of consumer goods to those who could afford to pay the high prices.*

THE END OF THE USSR

Gorbachev had set out with the intention of ending the Cold War but he was as surprised as the rest of the world at some of the consequences of his actions and decisions. He believed that the Communist states of the USSR and those in Eastern Europe could survive the end of the Cold War as a united body. Money spent on weapons, he planned, would be used instead to strengthen the Soviet economy and deliver a better standard of living for its citizens. Strict government controls would be relaxed, people would be happier, and a socialist USSR would co-exist peacefully with a capitalist America. What Gorbachev had not anticipated was that his reforms would lead to the break-up of the Soviet empire and the removal of its Communist governments.

? EVENT IN QUESTION

Did the USSR fall or was it pushed?

The Cold War did not come to an end because one side achieved a decisive military victory. The USA did, however, win an important economic victory in that it was more able than the USSR to support the huge cost of conducting the Cold War. From one viewpoint this proved that an economy like that of the USA, based on private ownership and profit, was better than an economy like the Soviet one that was based around state ownership. At the same time, it may have been the case that the USA deliberately set out to break the Soviet economy. Did the US increase the pace of the arms race so that the Soviet economy would be forced to try and keep up with it? This is hard to establish, one way or the other. In the early 1980s, however, the US did set out to weaken the Soviet economy by denying it trade with the West and holding back Western financial credit and new computer technology.

ABOVE *Boris Yeltsin, with papers in his hand, prepares to call upon Russians to reject the attempted seizure of power by Soviet conservatives in August 1991. Yeltsin eventually emerged as the new leader of post-Cold War Russia.*

'A COMMON VICTORY'

The last thing Gorbachev expected was for the USSR itself to break up and abandon Communism, yet this was what unfolded in 1991. Gorbachev and his supporters hoped that, once the Cold War was over, the West would be willing to aid the USSR in the form of large loans. This did not happen, making it more difficult for Gorbachev to deal with critics who felt that the USSR had made too many concessions to the West. On 19 August 1991, a group of Soviet conservatives seized power in Moscow, and Gorbachev, who was away on holiday, was placed under house arrest. The conservatives failed in their attempt, however, and Gorbachev was released. When he returned to Moscow he found that a new leader, Boris Yeltsin, had emerged.

Yeltsin now campaigned for the break-up of the USSR and a non-Communist government for an independent Russia. By the end of 1991, the USSR had ceased to exist as its various states, including Russia, became independent countries.

The Cold War ended, as it had begun, with a redrawing of Europe's map. Gorbachev, no longer a world leader, said at the beginning of 1992, 'I do not regard the end of the Cold War as a victory for one side ... The end of the Cold War is our common victory.' That may be true but for Gorbachev, who did so much to end the conflict, there was to be no place in a post-Cold War Europe.

? EVENT IN QUESTION

After the Cold War: is the world a safer place?

The fact that the Cold War is over, a part of history, might suggest that the world is now a safer place. Superpowers no longer threaten one another with missiles, nor do they fuel wars in various parts of the world in an attempt to weaken one another.

At the same time though, as Russia's leader Vladimir Putin said towards the end of 2001, 'The Cold War is over. The world has become much more complicated.' New international conflicts have arisen from the ashes of Cold War conflicts and, it could be argued, are more difficult to resolve because they cannot be controlled in the way they once were by the superpowers.

In the past, regional conflicts around the world were affected by the larger conflict between the USA and the USSR. The balance of power between the superpowers meant that neither side wanted a regional conflict to get out of control, and they acted to police such conflicts in ways that would benefit their own interests. Is the world safer without such a balance of power?

ABOVE *At the Cu Chi Revolutionary Martyrs Cemetery outside Ho Chi Minh City, Tran Thi Buon mourns at the grave of her husband, one of the victims of the Cold War, who died 34 years earlier while fighting US and South Vietnamese forces.*

COUNTING THE COST

It is hard to quantify the financial cost of the Cold War, but the superpowers stored many thousands of nuclear bombs and maintained huge armies of men and equipment. The USA, for example, was spending an average of $400 billion on its defence budget each year, and one estimate for the total cost to both sides of their weapons during the Cold War is $8 trillion ($8,000,000,000,000).

Another cost of the Cold War is measured in the number of human lives that it claimed. Millions of Koreans and Vietnamese died, over a million Afghans lost their lives, along with thousands of Soviet soldiers, fighting in Afghanistan, hundreds of thousands died in Angola, many tens of thousands in Central and South America. Thousands of people also died in Romania and Hungary. Russian tanks killed protestors in Czechoslovakia in 1968, and nearly 200 died trying to cross into West Berlin. Around a quarter of a million Chinese died in Korea, as well as more than 3,000 people of mainly British, Australian and Turkish nationality making up the UN force. Over 100,000 Americans died fighting foreign wars, and four American students died at Kent State University protesting against the Vietnam War.

? EVENT IN QUESTION

The avoidance of nuclear war: good judgement or good fortune?

What didn't happen in the Cold War – a nuclear war – is, in one sense, more important than what did happen. From the ruins of a devastated Europe in 1945, and an unstable Asia, two armed superpowers confronted one another. Each side was suspicious of the intentions of the other and they jostled uneasily for power in an uncertain world. The USA and the USSR learnt to respect each other's nuclear capabilities and became better at avoiding direct confrontation. Each side learnt to exercise caution and an uneasy world peace was maintained for over forty years. At the same time, though, many wars were fought and millions died all around the world. The fact that nuclear weapons were never used, it could be argued, was as much luck as anything else. There was always the possibility of an accident, a misunderstanding, or a deliberate choice, leading to someone pressing a button, releasing a nuclear missile and setting off a retaliatory attack.

THE LEGACY

Part of the cost of living through the Cold War was the general fear it created around the world that at any time a conflict situation involving the superpowers could develop into a crisis resulting in the use of nuclear weapons. The international, anti-nuclear peace movements that developed in the 1980s were a response to the climate of fear and uncertainty created in a world at the mercy of Cold War politics. The ending of the Cold War, a largely peaceful event, lifted this cloud of fear and

BELOW *The world was not necessarily a safer place. US Navy aircraft during training off the coast of Taiwan in 1996, as China began new live-fire war games in the Taiwan Strait.*

made the world seem a safer place. This is perhaps the greatest legacy of the Cold War.

But not every part of the world has shaken off its legacy from the Cold War. Korea remains a divided country and Cuba is still regarded with hostility by the USA. When China became independent in 1949, a small non-Communist force fled to the Chinese island of Taiwan and received support from America. The USA came to recognize Taiwan's claim to be an independent state, much to China's annoyance, and this remains an unresolved issue. The end of the Cold War has not brought peace to the world. The problems of the Middle East, and the fighting between the Palestinians and Israelis, have not been made any easier even though the Cold War is over. The Cold War is over but nuclear weapons still exist and could still be used. Indeed, there is now less control over the use of nuclear weapons than there was during the Cold War.

? EVENT IN QUESTION

A fight for freedom or a fight for power?

For some, the Cold War was a struggle between the USA's stand for freedom and what President Reagan called an 'evil empire'. It was a battle of ideas that saw the triumph of freedom when citizens pulled down the Berlin Wall. Other historians, pointing to the way in which democracies were overthrown and countries invaded by the US, regard this interpretation as very one-sided.

Some historians say that the two superpowers were much alike, agreeing to control different regions of the world and fighting wars whenever agreement could not be reached. Others argue that the USSR only wanted to defend itself and it was the USA who wanted to expand its power and influence. Was the Cold War a struggle between different belief systems or was it a struggle for power that ended when one economy proved the stronger? There can be no one explanation that simply explains the Cold War.

Timeline

1945
25 APRIL: American and Soviet soldiers meet on the Elbe river in Germany.

1945
7 MAY: Germany surrenders and World War II comes to an end in Europe.

1945
6 and 9 AUGUST: Atom bombs dropped on two Japanese cities.

1945
2 SEPTEMBER: Japan surrenders and World War II comes to an end in Asia.

1948
18 JUNE: A new currency for western Germany introduced.

1948
22 JUNE: A new currency for eastern Germany introduced.

1948
24 JUNE: The blockade of Berlin begins and, two days later, the first airlift arrives in western Berlin.

1949
12 MAY: The blockade of Berlin is lifted by the Soviet Union.

1949
1 OCTOBER: China becomes an independent country.

1950
25 JUNE: South Korea invaded by North Korea.

1953
27 JULY: A ceasefire signals the end of the Korean War.

1954
JUNE: The government of Guatemala is overthrown by a CIA-trained guerrilla force and a military government is established.

1956
NOVEMBER: Hungarian uprising crushed by Soviet forces.

1959
8 JANUARY: Castro forms a new government in Cuba after the overthrow of a dictatorship.

1961
13 AUGUST: East Germany decides to begin building a barrier between East and West Berlin. This becomes the Berlin Wall.

1961
13 APRIL: A failed invasion of Cuba, planned by the CIA, gets underway.

1962
14 OCTOBER: US spy plane photographs missile sites under construction in Cuba.

1962
27 OCTOBER: Kennedy and Khruschev come to a peaceful agreement over Cuba and the Soviet missiles are withdrawn.

1965
FEBRUARY: Heavy US bombing of North Vietnam begins.

1965
APRIL: US invasion of Dominican Republic.

1967
JUNE: The Six-Day War between Israel and the Arab states of Egypt, Jordan and Syria.

1968
MARCH: United States announces decision to withdraw from Vietnam and seek peace.
AUGUST: Soviet forces intervene in Czechoslovakia.

1969
NOVEMBER: Strategic Arms Limitation Talks (SALT) begin in Helsinki.

1972
FEBRUARY: President Nixon meets Mao Zedong in China.

1973
11 SEPTEMBER: President Allende of Chile is killed and General Pinochet becomes head of a military government.

1973
SEPTEMBER: President Allende of Chile overthrown in a coup.

1973
OCTOBER: The October War, or Yom Kippur War, between Israel, Egypt and Syria.

1975
APRIL: North Vietnam takes over South Vietnam and the country is unified.

1975
NOVEMBER: Civil war in Angola and an invasion by South African troops is defeated by Cuban forces.

1979
JUNE: After a civil war, a Sandinista government is formed in Nicaragua.

1979
DECEMBER: The Soviet invasion of Afghanistan begins.

1981
NOVEMBER: The CIA begins training and arming the Contras to fight the Sandinista government in Nicaragua.

1983
MARCH: President Reagan announces 'Star Wars' missile defence system.

1983
OCTOBER: USA military intervention in Grenada.

1989
FEBRUARY: Soviet troops withdraw from Afghanistan.

1989
AUGUST: A non-Communist government is formed in Poland.

1989
9 NOVEMBER: The Berlin Wall comes down.

1990
OCTOBER: East and West Germany reunited.

1991
AUGUST: Failed attempt to overthrow Gorbachev in Moscow.

1991
DECEMBER: The USSR ceases to exist.

Glossary

Allies The countries at war against Germany, Japan and their supporters in World War II.

armoury A range of weapons.

arms race A competitive race to develop better weapons.

capitalist Supporting the economic system of capitalism, based upon private ownership and the pursuit of profits.

CIA The Central Intelligence Agency of the US, a state-funded organization.

colonial Relating to a colony, a country ruled and inhabited by people of a foreign government.

communism The political and economic system of the USSR and Eastern Europe during the Cold War, based around one-party rule and state control of the economy.

congress The part of the US government that passes new laws.

conservatives In politics, people who don't want to make changes.

dictatorship A state under the control of a ruler with unlimited authority.

diplomatic relations Peaceful channels of communication between countries through embassies.

Eastern Europe During the Cold War this referred to European countries that had Communist governments and were supported by the USSR.

guerrilla war A war between an independent, and usually political, force and larger regular forces, often representing a government.

Iron Curtain A term that came to describe the closed border between Eastern and Western Europe during the Cold War.

KGB The USSR's state-funded organization for the country's security, operating within the USSR and through foreign countries; established to help conduct the Cold War.

labour camp A prison camp based around and enforcing hard labour.

left wing Socialist.

liberal reforms The relaxation of laws, usually economic and social laws that are regarded as too strict.

medium range nuclear missiles Nuclear weapons capable of travelling a medium range, within a continent rather than between continents.

Mujahedeen Islamic fighters who resisted the Soviet occupation of Afghanistan between 1979 and 1989.

national security advisor A person appointed to inform and advise the US president on matters of national security.

nationalist patriot A person with principles supporting a policy of national independence.

nationalize To take over the private ownership of an industry or business on behalf of the State.

NATO North Atlantic Treaty Organization, formed by the West to conduct the Cold War.

Nazism The political and racist system of Hitler's Germany between 1933 and 1945.

pacifist someone who believes that war and violence are not a solution to disputes, and that they can be settled by peaceful means.

patriotism A strong and devoted support to a country.

Further information

propaganda Information, or misinformation, designed to present only one point of view.

retaliatory Responding to an attack by launching a counter-attack of a similar kind.

revolution Far-reaching change, often involving the overthrow of a government or a social order.

Russia *see* USSR.

SALT Strategic Arms Limitation Talks, starting with SALT-1 in the early 1970s.

socialism A left wing, non-Communist, set of political and social ideas.

superpower A state with supreme power and influence, like the USA and the USSR during the Cold War.

supply lines Routes used for providing supplies and weapons during a war.

Taliban The Islamic group that emerged strong enough to form a government, after Afghanistan's civil war following the withdrawal of Soviet troops.

United Nations An international peace-seeking organization made up of representatives of most of the world's states.

USSR The Union of Socialist Soviet Republics, the Communist state set up in 1917 and disbanded at the end of 1991.

Warsaw Pact Formed by the USSR and Eastern Europe to conduct the Cold War, equivalent of NATO in the West.

the West In international politics, countries like the USA, many European states, and Japan. The Cold War pitted the West against the East (the USSR and Eastern Europe).

BOOKS

S. Adam, *The Cold War* (Franklin Watts, 2001)

Bob Fowke, *The Cold War* (Hodder Children's Books, 2001)

Christine Hatt, *The End of the Cold War* (Hodder Wayland, 2002)

Jeremy Isaacs and Taylor Downing, *The Cold War* (Transworld Publishing Ltd, 1998)

Peter J Kuznick and James Gilbert (eds.), *Rethinking Cold War Culture* (Smithsonian Institution Press, 2001)

Klaus Larres and Ann Lane (eds.), *The Cold War* (Blackwell, 2001)

Priscella Roberts, *The Cold War* (Sutton Publishing Ltd, 2000)

Stewart Ross, *The Cold War: Causes* (Hodder Wayland, 2001)

Joseph Smith, *The Cold War* (Blackwell, 1989)

David Taylor, *20th Century Perspectives: The Cold War* (Heinemann Library, 2001)

Martin Walker, *The Cold War* (Henry Holt & Company, Inc., 1993)

Index

Raintree is an imprint of Capstone Global Library
Limited, a company incorporated in England and Wales
having its registered office at 7 Pilgrim Street, London,
EC4V GLB – Registered company number: 6695582

www.raintreepublishers.co.uk
myorders@raintreepublishers.co.uk

First published by Raintree in 2014
The moral rights of the proprietor have been asserted.

Originally published by DC Comics in the U.S. in single
magazine form as Teen Titans GO! #2. Copyright © 2013
DC Comics. All Rights Reserved.

Ashley C. Andersen Zantop *Publisher*
Michael Dahl *Editorial Director*
Sean Tulien *Editor*
Heather Kindseth *Creative Director*
Alison Thiele *Designer*
Kathy McColley *Production Specialist*

DC COMICS
Kristy Quinn *Original U.S. Editor*

ISBN 978 1 406 27948 1

Printed in China by Nordica.
1013/CA21301918
17 16 15 14 13
10 9 8 7 6 5 4 3 2 1

A full catalogue record for this book
is available from the British Library.

TEEN TITANS GO!

MY CRUMMY VALENTINE

J. Torres	writer
John McCrea & James Hodgkins	artists
Brad Anderson	colourist
Jared K. Fletcher	letterer

TEEN TITANS GO!

ROBIN

REAL NAME: Dick Grayson

BIO: The perfectionist leader of the group has one main complaint about his teammates: the other Titans just won't do what he says. As the partner of Batman, Robin is a talented acrobat, martial artist, and hacker.

STARFIRE

REAL NAME: Princess Koriand'r

BIO: Formerly a warrior Princess of the now-destroyed planet Tamaran, Starfire found a new home on Earth, and a new family in the Teen Titans.

CYBORG

REAL NAME: Victor Stone

BIO: Cyborg is a laid-back half teen, half robot who's more interested in eating pizza and playing video games than fighting crime.

RAVEN

REAL NAME: Raven

BIO: Raven is an Azarathian empath who can teleport and control her "soul-self," which can fight physically as well as act as Raven's eyes and ears away from her body.

BEAST BOY

REAL NAME: Garfield Logan

BIO: Beast Boy is Cyborg's best bud. He's a slightly dim but lovable loafer who can transform into all sorts of animals [when he's not too busy eating burritos and watching TV]. He's also a vegetarian.

9

11

12

TITANS GO!

CYBORG! YOU ARE THE ONE WHO TOLD ME ALL ABOUT THE WONDERS OF THE VALENTINE'S DAY--

BEAST BOY! IT'S ME--

KYAI!

HOO
FISH

SMACK

GET UP!
I **COMMAND** YOU
TO GET UP!

I THOUGHT IT WAS THE
VALENTINE'S DAY, NOT THE
VILLAIN-TIME'S DAY!

NOW, STARFIRE!
WE NEED TO GET
TO 'EM WHILE
THEY'RE STILL
DAZED!

CREATORS

J. TORRES WRITER

J. Torres won the Shuster Award for Outstanding Writer for his work on Batman: Legends of the Dark Knight, Love As a Foreign Language, and Teen Titans Go! He is also the writer of the Eisner Award nominated Alison Dare and the YALSA listed Days Like This and Lola: A Ghost Story. Other comic book credits include Avatar: The Last Airbender, Batman: The Brave and the Bold, Legion of Super-Heroes in the 31st Century, Ninja Scroll, Wonder Girl, Wonder Woman, and WALL-E: Recharge.

JOHN MCCREA ARTIST

John McCrea has illustrated iconic entities like Batman, Superman, Wonder Woman, and many others. He also does design work and story-boarding, and he's a Lucasfilm accredited artist.

JAMES HODGKINS ARTIST

James Hodgkins has a background in graphic design and has done illustration work for advertising, film, and comic books. Officially accredited by LucasFilms, James is one of few artists approved to produce official Star Wars material.

GLOSSARY

affection – a great liking for someone, or the act of showing it

bewildering – confusing

bidding – if you do someone's bidding, you follow their orders

chaperone – adult who protects young people and makes sure they behave themselves

consult – go to a person for advice

contrived – obviously fake

dazed – stunned or unable to think clearly

emit – release or send out something like light or heat

gondola – a light boat with high, pointed ends that is moved through the water with a long pole

ironic – using words to express a meaning that is the opposite of its literal meaning

spectacle – remarkable and dramatic sight

VISUAL QUESTIONS & PROMPTS

1. In this panel, Robin uses his smarts and skills to defeat a foe he doesn't want to hurt. What are some other ways Robin uses his skills to solve problems in this book?

2. Beast Boy can shape-shift into any animal he likes. What kinds of animals might be helpful in fighting crime?

3. Sometimes panels in comic books show a sequence of events in one panel. Describe what sequence of events is happening to Beast Boy in this panel.

3

...PEOPLE EXCHANGE CARDS AND WRITE LOVE POEMS AND GO ON ROMANTIC DATES AND SEND EACH OTHER FLOWERS--

AND GIVE EACH OTHER CANDY AND CHOCOLATES AND PIZZA!

NICE WORK, RAVEN! HOWEVER... WHERE HAVE YOU BEEN ALL DAY?

NOWHERE... DOING NOTHING... WITH NO ONE.

4. Why would Raven not want to tell Starfire (or anyone else) what she was doing on Valentine's Day? Explain your answer.

LOOKS LIKE SOMEONE'S BEEN GETTIN' THEIR VALENTINE ON!

4

GRR...

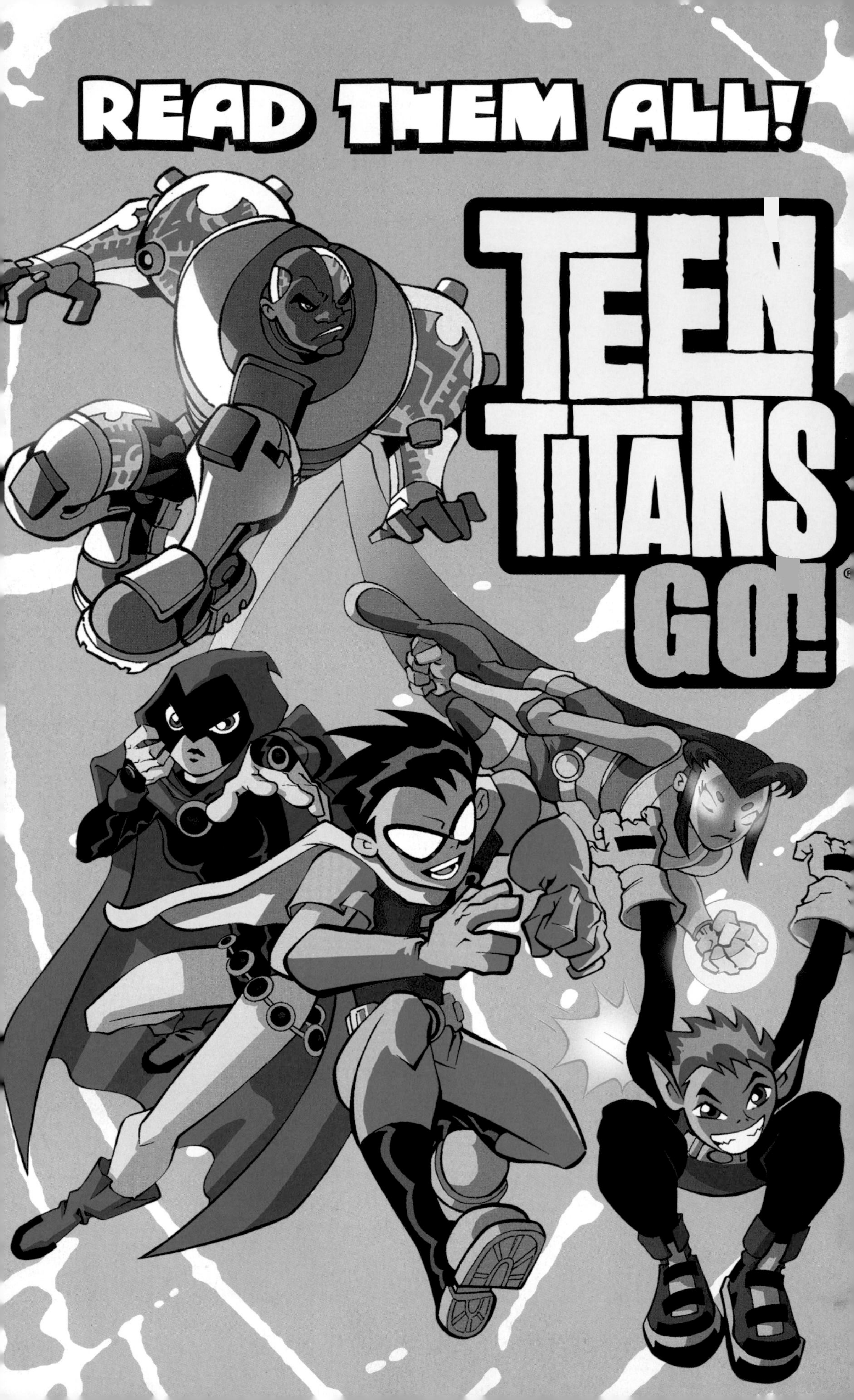
READ THEM ALL!
TEEN TITANS GO!